Praise for *How to Sell Anything to Anyone Anytime*

"Everyone is in sales in some form, and Dave Kahle blends theory and practice to provide a well-organized primer on the science and art of selling that anyone can understand and put into action."

—Deirdre Jones, associate director, Edward H. Schmidt School of Professional Sales Marketing and International Business Department, College of Business Administration, University of Toledo

"This is not your typical book on 'selling strategies.' This book is about employing a well-structured approach to providing your customers with a credible, value-enhancing business relationship— a relationship built on a foundation of trust—and then actually delivering something to your customers that makes them better. Follow Dave's road map, and both you and your customers will benefit from it."

—Tom B. Highley, CEO, Tenon Limited

"Incredibly powerful in its dissection of the critical path to success in sales! This book will revolutionize your thinking on sales and how you can really sell anything to anybody anytime!"

—Thomas Sudyk, CEO, Ec Group International

"This book makes me want to be 20 again just starting out. It is amazing to me how many times a day it comes back to me when I am talking to people and give them advice that was in the book. Once published, I will buy one for every sales person and every sales manager we have. If you can't win after reading this, you need to be doing something else with your time."

—Doug Rathbun, senior executive vice president of sales
and marketing, Lumbermen's, Inc.

"Don't tell my competitors about this book! It's packed with simple, timeless principles that are applicable to any product. Any service. Anywhere. It's a must-read for anyone that wants to sell something."

—Greg Underwood, director of sales, Virbac Animal Health

"As usual, common-sense, practical, easy-to-use advice from Dave Kahle that can be implemented the moment you set the book down to improve your sales results. Well worth the read."

—John Koeble, vice president of sales,
Continental Packaging Solutions

"Simple yet profound sales advice. Destined to become a classic."
—Charles Robinson, CEO, WISE Ministries International

"This book is a great read for every level of sales professional. If you have been in sales for 30 days or 30 years, you will get something out of this book. Follow the system and your sales will grow!"

—Steve Coen, WinWholesale, vice president, Western Region

HOW TO SELL ANYTHING TO ANYONE ANYTIME

By Dave Kahle

CAREER PRESS

Pompton Plains, NJ

HOW TO SELL ANYTHING TO ANYONE ANYTIME
EDITED BY GINA HOOGERHYDE
TYPESET BY DIANA GHAZZAWI
Cover design by Wes Youssi/M80 Design
Printed in the U.S.A.

To order this title, please call toll-free 1-800-CAREER-1 (NJ and Canada:
201-848-0310) to order using VISA or MasterCard, or for further information on books from Career Press.

The Career Press, Inc.
220 West Parkway, Unit 12
Pompton Plains, NJ 07444
www.careerpress.com

Library of Congress Cataloging-in-Publication Data
Kahle, Dave.
    How to sell anything to anyone anytime / by Dave Kahle.
        p. cm.
    Includes index.
        ISBN 978-1-60163-131-2--ISBN 978-1-60163-718-5 (ebook) 1. Selling.
    2. Sales management. I. Title.

HF5438.25.K336 2011
658.85--dc22
                                                    2010025456

Acknowledgments

I've written a number of other books, but with this one, more so than the others, I feel a much greater need to acknowledge a whole slew of people.

I'm reminded of my father, who died far too young. He provided me a role model of a professional sales person before I even knew what a sales person was.

Then, of course, there is every sales manager and company who ever hired me to sell for them: Jewel Companies, H.C. Electronics, U.S. Surgical Corp, Greening & Hoffman, and White & White. They provided the experience and guidance that laid the foundation for my second career.

Since 1988 I have served hundreds of clients, helping them increase their sales and develop their people. Every single one of them signed a contract and wrote a check. These engagements provided me with the opportunity to practice my craft, assist them in growing their businesses, and further refine the ideas expressed in this book.

Thousands of people have attended presentations at conventions and conferences and interacted with me at Webinars and seminars around the continent. The feedback they provided throughout the years provided the knife that helped me carve out the superfluous from this program, and whittle and shape the message.

My staff, particularly Cheryl, who read every word, has provided me the time and space to write this book.

My wife, Coleen, is forever supportive.

My Savior, Jesus Christ, has transformed my life and brought me to a place where I can touch people with expertise and authority.

I owe them all.

Contents

Introduction

So, you want to sell something. Maybe you want to sell yourself to a prospective employer, or maybe you want to start an internet business, open a coffee shop at the corner strip mall, or make more money in your current sales position.

There is a fundamental sales process that applies to every selling situation—regardless of what you need to sell, to whom you need to sell it, or the method or medium you need to use. If you can understand and master that selling process, you'll be able to sell anything to anyone—not every time, but often enough to make you successful.

Do you remember what the first Iraq war did to the economy? The layoffs spiked, unemployment went through the roof, and nobody wanted to spend money.

However, a 50 year-old shoe store wanted to try to buck the trend. Together, we applied some of the principles and practices you'll learn in this book. In a depressed economy, when people all around him were cutting back and slimming down, he had the following year over year increases:

- March: 18.4%
- April: 13.7%
- May: 14.2%
- June: 10.1%
- July: 19.0%
- August: 15.4%

I know that you are probably thinking that the Iraq war was a long time ago, but that's precisely my point. In the world of selling, there are timeless universal principles, processes, and practices that can be successfully applied to any product and any market at any time.

Those individuals who recognize and implement those principles, processes, and practices are far more successful than those who don't. Not only can you learn the ageless truths of selling, but you can forever improve your ability to implement them. That's the premise of this book.

I know what you're thinking: Can "sales" really be that simple? YES. Regardless of what countless sales books proclaim, selling is not magic, and there are no secrets. Instead, there are identifiable, understandable, reproducible steps in the process which, when implemented with some degree of proficiency, can be expected to lead to a positive outcome.

Throughout my adult life, I have continually sold something. My first real selling experience was during the summer of my college years when I was selling groceries and household items to housewives during the summers of my college years.

From that I moved on to selling men's suits and sport coats in a retail clothing store. Next, I sold amplification equipment to classrooms of hearing-impaired children, I sold surgical staplers to surgeons, and from there I moved on to self-improvement products, sales recruiting (selling people), and then on to 40,000 different items with a wholesale distributor.

In my career as a salesperson working for someone else, I have been the number-one salesperson in the country for two different companies in two distinctly different selling situations and markets.

For the last 20-plus years, I've had my own business, training tens of thousands of salespeople in a wide variety of industries and products—everything from sophisticated million-dollar pieces of production machinery to $2 hot packs. I've worked with bosses, owners, and sales executives to help them design and implement more effective sales systems. I've written seven books and hundreds of articles on selling. Sometimes it feels as though I have literally been a part of selling almost everything to almost everyone.

In all of these various sales experiences, I have observed what I call the Kahle Way Sales Process. I don't make any claims that I invented it, or even discovered it. I have just observed it and put it together in a way that makes it easy for you to use.

It's sort of like gardening. If you want to have a batch of carrots to enjoy a couple of months from now, you must first find a spot of ground that looks relatively fertile. Then you must clear that space, select good seeds, plant them at an appropriate depth and time of year, be sure they receive enough water, and prevent too much competition from the weeds. If you do all that, you have every right to expect a harvest of good carrots.

Notice that no one invented the process to grow carrots. The process that you followed to reap the harvest was a combination of a series of observations that people have made throughout the years as to how carrots grow.

You put that series of observations together into a process, and that process leads you to an understanding of what you must do to enjoy fresh carrots.

The fundamental sales process is like that. It's not that anyone (including me) invented it. It is more of a series of observations about how people buy, put together into a process. The facts are the facts, the observations are the observations. If you want to sell something, this is how you do it. If you implement the process, you have every right to expect a harvest.

My role, and the role of this book, is to describe the process in such a way that it will be easy for you to understand and easy for you to implement.

My goal is that, by the time you are finished reading it, you will understand that process, and be equipped to sell anything to anyone anytime.

—

1

And You Thought Sales Was All About...

My wife, like so many other people, has an aversion to salespeople. When a salesperson approaches her in a retail store, she heads in the opposite direction. I'm not sure why she feels this way, but I do know she shares some of those feelings with lots of other people.

If you are one of those people, we need to deal with that before we go any further. If you have negative ideas and feelings about salespeople and selling in general, those ideas can spill over and influence the quality of your work as you attempt to sell something. You may be thinking, for example, "I could never be a salesperson!" Why do you think that?

It is probably because you have some idea, some picture in your mind, of what a salesperson is, and you find yourself not quite matching that picture. It would not be un-usual if that picture took root in some negative experience that you had in the past—maybe a really pushy automobile salesperson, or the guy who came to the house to sell you home improvements and you just couldn't get rid of him.

Believe me, there are enough bad examples of irritating salespeople in this world to populate all of our bad dreams for quite some time. They are the source for lots of common-ly held misconceptions about salespeople and about selling. Let's explore some of them.

Misconception: Salespeople are glad-handing, outgoing people and therefore, to sell something, you must fit into that mold.

Like a lot of misconceptions, there is a grain of truth in this one. Most professional salespeople are people-oriented. In other words, they are social people who like to be around others. In terms of the sheer numbers, more professional salespeople would fall into that category than any other category.

But that doesn't necessarily prescribe a personality type for success in sales. From my personal experience, many of the best salespeople are introverts who spend a lot of time in thought, so that their time in front of the customer is highly effective. I have known excellent salespeople of every pos-sible personality type.

It's not the personality type that determines a successful salesperson; it is his/her understanding and application of the core principles, processes, and practices of effective sales. People become effective in sales not because of the personal-ity traits with which they started, but rather because of the practices to which they adhered.

And besides, you don't necessarily want to become a salesperson, you just want to help people buy.

Misconception: Salespeople are good talkers.

There is absolutely not even a pebble of truth in this one. In fact, the truth lies in the opposite extreme. Good salespeople are good *listeners,* and the best salespeople listen more effectively than the rest of the world.

Salespeople who do all of the talking are usually not very good salespeople. Of course, that's easy to understand. If we are going to help people buy, we must listen to what they say, so that we can understand what they want. That's just good common sense.

Misconception: I must thoroughly know the product if I am going to sell it.

Here's one with a seed of truth in it. Of course it is helpful to know the product, but a deep and detailed knowledge of all of the features of a product is hardly a prerequisite for the ability to sell it. For example, I sold lots of suits and sport coats in my days of selling in a retail men's store without knowing much about them. I honestly couldn't tell you where they were made, what type of material they were composed of, and so on. However, I could tell you which one looked the best on you, and what each did for your image.

You see, the salesperson stands between the customer and the product or service that meets the customer's needs. Although it may be helpful to know a lot about the product, and there are some technical sales situations where it is important to understand many of the technical details, it's far more important to concentrate on the customer, and know a lot about him or her.

In fact, knowing too much about the product can be a detriment to a successful salesperson. It leads you to focus on the product, not the customer. It tempts you with the allure of being the "encyclopedia" of information, and lures you into long-winded dissertations on the intricacies of the product. I never will forget a training session in which the salesperson droned on and on about the product, purging every possible detail out of his mind. As he went on and on he was oblivious to the customer, who actually started to fall asleep, which is a perfect example of product knowledge crowding out sensitivity to the customer.

In my tenure as a salesperson, I have sold lots of things that I didn't know much about. In some cases, I sold things for which I had absolutely no firsthand knowledge. In fact, I have sold things that I didn't even know what they were!

Misconception: I must believe in a product or service before I could sell it.

This is a tough one, because it sounds so reasonable. How could you possibly sell something in which you didn't believe? Wouldn't that be horribly dishonest—the worst kind of sales hypocrisy that gives rise to all these negative ideas?

No. Stick with me on this. This misconception holds that the product, or more specifically, the salesperson's opinion of the product, is the ultimate influencer of sales behavior. The salesperson's opinion becomes more important than the needs and situation of the customer.

Why should your opinion be superior to the customers' opinion? You see, the point is that my (or any salesperson's) opinion should not take precedence over the customer's needs. It puts the wrong issue at the heart of the sales process. When you hold this belief, the sale is not about the customers' situations, opinions, and needs; it's about your opinion of the product.

Who gave you such omnipotent insight? Where did you acquire such absolute judgment? Where did you gain such arrogance as to think your opinion was superior?

If you are going to help the customer buy, you must work on the assumption that your opinion is secondary to the customer's opinion. Your job is to find out what the customer wants, and show him that what you have gives him what he wants. You don't need to believe your product is the best; you just need to understand what the customer wants and how your product gives him what he wants.

All of these are misconceptions that hinder people from undertaking a sales effort. If you hold any of them, they may subtly prevent you from being as successful in your sales efforts as you could be.

The truth is that sales is a process, and anyone with just a smattering of people skills, the drive to learn, and the willingness to follow through on their plans, can learn to implement that process.

Although anyone can learn the sales process and be somewhat effective, everyone can do it better. And doing sales better is absolutely critical to the success of any endeavor, whether it be an individual trying to find freelance jobs, the new corner coffeeshop, or the sophisticated B2B seller.

When the economy is growing, you don't need to be nearly as good. All you have to do is show up and be moderately competent at what you do. In a declining economy, you have to be better. You must sell, and sell better, which brings us to the misconception that is the single biggest killer of success in the business world I have ever come across. This toxic idea is a killer.

Misconception: If I offer a quality product or service, people will come to me and I don't need to sell effectively.

I think this misconception is responsible for more failed business efforts than any other single idea. It probably arises from that often repeated bit of conventional un-wisdom: Build a better mousetrap, and the world will beat a path to your door.

Nothing is further from the truth. A better mousetrap, a high-quality product, or an effective service is just the first step, not the entire strategy. I cannot tell you how many people I have met who had spent huge amounts of time, effort, money, and emotional involvement in the development of an idea, only to have nothing left to invest in the selling, and therefore crashed and burned when it didn't sell.

The economic landscape is littered with the carcasses of failed endeavors built around the premise that "If you do it better, people will buy it." The owners and entrepreneurs who started them never understood the most important part of the equation: you must also sell it effectively.

The world is full of freelancers, craftsmen, and for-hire professionals who are perfectly capable of providing a quality product or service, in many cases at lower prices than the market. Graphic designers, writers, management consultants, plumbers, painters, and carpenters all share the same obstacles. Despite their ability to perform the service, the overwhelming majority eek out a living, existing from one paycheck to the next, never fully reaching their potential. Why? Because in spite of their ability to deliver a quality service, they don't know how to sell that service. And selling the service is more difficult and more important than delivering it.

Now, I know I have just incurred the wrath of countless engineers and designers who have worked extremely hard to create the next new thing. I am not demeaning your skills nor discounting the hard work you have put in. But in the big picture the success of a business effort—particularly a new one—is more dependent on the sales effort than anything else.

Here's an example: I was approached by a small company who had invested about three years of development into the creation of a new product. The product was ready. The problem was, of course, they were having problems selling it.

I discovered that the product was purchased by a segment of the market that they did not call upon. They did all their work with contractors, and this was a product that was specified by architects. It didn't fit their current market. They had not calculated that into the equation when they created the new product. Instead, the owner had become enamored with the idea of the product, and had invested much of his company's resources into its development. This product could not be sold through their current methods, relationships, and people. Now, they had no money left for the creation of a sales effort.

I could do nothing for them. They struggled for years after that, burdened by the time, money, and energy costs of creating a new product without considering the efforts necessary to sell that product. I could go on and on with examples of people who were good at something, or who made a good product or offered a service and thought that was all they needed to do to be successful.

If I were to have given them advice at the beginning of their efforts, the advice would be this: Before you make it, figure out how you are going to sell it. And, if you can't sell it, and sell it better than the next guy, don't make it.

Selling it is the hard part. But with the information in this book, you'll be able to sell anything.

2

Simplifying the Fundamental Sales Process

Now that I've punctured your misconceptions about what sales is, and given you some ideas about what sales is not, it's time to hone in on the good stuff. Here are three different definitions to help you come to grips with what selling really entails.

1. Selling is the science of helping people get what they want.

If your prospective customer doesn't want or need what you are offering—if it doesn't fill some need for the customer—then you have no business engaging in the selling process with him or her. Now don't get too hung up on the definition of "need." If we define that too narrowly, it would eliminate everything except food and shelter. Our needs and wants are always expanding, and include things that make us feel good or fill some emotional need, as well those that meet our basic needs. We may not really need a caramel cream latte, but thousands are purchased every day.

Although selling is what you do, and you can do it better, it is still less about you and more about your customer.

2. Selling is the process of helping people make decisions that often lead them to purchase from you.

Effective selling begins with an understanding that it is about influencing the decisions of the customer. In other words, the ultimate location for the sales process is the mind and heart of the customer. Very few sales situations involve only one decision. One decision leads to another, which leads to another, which leads to the decision to buy.

Here's an example I often use to illustrate this point. Let's take one of the simplest selling situations with which I have ever been involved: selling water softeners to homeowners. This is a classic "one-call close." In other words, there is only one sales call necessary to help the customer make a decision. You either sell it when you see them, or you don't sell it at all.

It sounds simple, but even that simple, one-call sales process is quite a bit more involved when examined through the perspective of the decisions that the customer must make. Look at the following illustration.

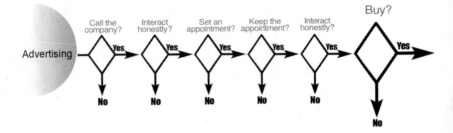

To initiate the process, the company must advertise and make it appear to be a reputable solution for hard water problems. The customer lives in the land of apathy and ignorance. In other words, they don't know the salesperson or the company, and that's fine with them. Their life is okay without them. So, they are ignorant of the company and apathetic about it.

The first decision the customer must make is whether or not to call the company. The company hopes to influence that decision by the quality of its advertising, as well as its reputation in the market.

Let's say the customer decides in the affirmative, and calls the company. Now, the customer has a salesperson on the phone. The customer now must make a decision as to whether or not to interact honestly with the salesperson. If the salesperson seems rude, arrogant, or uninterested, the customer may decide to call someone else. Some get that impression, and terminate the call. Others decide that the salesperson sounds trustworthy and competent, and so they continue the conversation.

As the conversation progresses, the salesperson is going to ask the customer for an appointment to come out, look at their situation, and test the water. Another decision for the customer.

Some decide not to do that for whatever reason, and they drop out of the process. Others decide to make the appointment, and move one step closer in the process.

Now, the customer faces yet another decision: whether or not to keep the appointment. Somewhere around 20 to 30 percent of those who make appointments decide after the fact not to keep it. So, they make sure they are gone when the salesperson shows up, or they hide in the basement and wait until he leaves. Those who do not keep the appointment drop out of the process, and those who decide to keep it move one step further along.

The salesperson shows up, this time in person, in the customer's home. The customer has to decide whether or not to be honest and forthcoming with the salesperson. Should she let me test the water? Should she take him down in the basement and show him the old equipment? If the salesperson appears competent and trustworthy, she will generally decide to interact honestly and the process moves along.

Finally, the salesperson tests the water, makes a recommendation for a new system, and asks the customer to buy.

This simple one-call close selling process consisted of a series of six decisions. Even in this simple selling process, the effective salesperson understands that it is a series of decisions, and his or her job is to help the customer make each affirmatively.

3. Selling is both simple and incredibly challenging.

It is simple in that almost every adult of reasonable intelligence, who has just a modicum of people skills, can understand it and do it. However, it is incredibly challenging to become exceptionally good at it, and it takes a lifetime of effort and practice.

Here's an example. Let's compare selling to the game of basketball. Anyone can take a basketball, bounce it a couple of times, and throw it at a hoop. In its essence, that's the game of basketball. However, there is a great distance between the skills and competence of the novice and those of someone like LeBron James. Although the world is full of people who can play basketball, only a handful compete at a world class level.

The Kahle Way Selling Process

Here's the process described briefly. As we go through the book, we'll dig deeper into each of the steps, and I'll show you how each step can be used in a variety of mediums and selling situations.

Step 1: Engage with the right people

"Engage" means to interact in some kind of communication. It can be face-to-face, over the phone, through e-mail, or via a Website. "Right people" means those people who have a need or interest in your product, and for whom the timing is right.

If you don't engage with the right people, you spend all of your time in the wrong place. Sort of like trying to plant your carrot seeds on a cement sidewalk. You can do everything else right, but it won't matter.

Step 2: Make them comfortable with you

If they are going to believe what you say, you have to be somewhat credible, and they have to feel at least a little bit comfortable with you. If they aren't comfortable with you, they won't spend much time with you, and the time that they do spend will be guarded and tentative. It doesn't matter if it's on a Website, or in a face-to-face encounter. They may be convinced to do business with you because of the fundamental attractiveness of your offer, but if they are not comfortable with you, it will be action taken against the grain. They will be forever uncomfortable and eager to find a replacement.

On the other hand, if they are comfortable with you, they won't mind spending time with you. They'll be much more open to sharing the information that is necessary for you to do a good job of crafting a solution. They'll believe what you have to say. You'll get the benefit of the doubt and they'll be eager to share future opportunities with you.

Step 3: Find out what they want

Selling is not manipulating people so that they take something they don't want. It is, instead, finding out what they already want, and appealing to that interest. The best salespeople excel at this step in the process.

I believe this step is the heart of selling—the essence of what sales is all about. I know that flies in the face of the routine practices of multitudes of salespeople, who believe that the end all of their focus is to push their product.

You can proclaim the merits of your product to willing and unwilling listeners and Webpage visitors far and wide, attempting to sway them with the powerful features and advantages that your product offers better than the competition. Or you can focus on the customer, finding out what motivates him, what issues are important to her, what problems he has, what objectives she is trying to solve, what he looks for in a vendor, and so on.

Everything that comes before is designed to get to this understanding. And everything that you do after is based on this step. It is the fulcrum upon which the entire sales process pivots.

Step 4: Show them how what you have gives them what they want

Proclaiming your product's features is the preferred routine of the mediocre salesperson. Personally and individually crafting your presentation to show the customer how what you have gives him what he wants is the mindset that, in part, defines the master salespeople.

If what you have doesn't help them get what they want, you either have the wrong thing, or you are talking to the wrong person. See how simple this is?

Step 5: Gain an agreement on the next step

Closing the sale is by far the most over-hyped phase of selling. If you have the right person, uncovered something they want, and you have shown them how what you have gives them what they want, why wouldn't he or she take the next positive step? It's natural. You just need to help the customer define what that is, and commit to it.

In a simple, direct-to-the-consumer sale, the next step is typically to buy the product. However, in more complex sales, there can be a series of appropriate next steps. They may need to test it, evaluate it, and submit it to a committee.

Every sales interaction has an assumed next step. If you call someone for an appointment, the next step is the appointment. If you present your solution to a decision-maker, the next step is the order. In between, there are thousands of potentially different sales calls, and thousands of potential action steps that follow the sales call.

The agreement is the ultimate rationale for the sales call and the aspect that makes it a "sales" call. A sales call is set apart from the rest of the interactions in this world by the fact that it anticipates an agreement. Without an agreement, the process has been a waste of time. It is the ultimate goal of every salesperson, and of every sales process, and of every sales call.

Step 6: Follow up and leverage the transaction to other opportunities

After they buy, you then make sure that they were satisfied, and you assume that, because they are satisfied, they will want to do other business with you and will want to let their friends know about you as well.

This is the step of the sales process that is most commonly neglected. Most salespeople are so focused on making the sale they neglect to consider that their real purpose is to satisfy the customer. And that extends beyond just the sale itself.

The sales call on the customer, made after the sale is complete, delivered and implemented by the customer, is one of the most powerful sales calls available. In it, the salesperson seeks assurance that the customer is satisfied, and then leverages that affirmation to uncover additional opportunities within the customer and/or referrals to people in other organizations.

The Kahle Way Sales Process Illustrated

Here's a graphic representation of the process. Notice, first, that each step occurs within the framework of the "right people." In other words, if you do all the right things, but do them with the wrong people, you're not even on the diagram. It's an exercise in futility and a waste of your time.

Notice that making them comfortable with you, is in the center of the diagram, touching every other step. Although it must happen early in the sales process, it must be continually nurtured throughout the process. At any point in the process, your customer can grow leery or irritated with you, and that disrupts everything.

You can do each step better

It's one thing to be able to do each step, and it's another to be able to do each step better! Just like every other field of human endeavor, there are the average performers, and there are those who do it better!

Here's an example. I love to golf. But I am, at best, an average golfer. I'm not nearly as good as many of the golfers in my league. I know I have the potential to golf better—after all, many of them get better every year. But, alas, I just don't have the time and energy to put into becoming better. So, while I am an average golfer, I could, if I chose, become better.

This is the same point with every one of these steps in the process. There is adequate performance, and then there is better performance. But it's not an either/or kind of situation. There are degrees of better. There's lots of room between me and Tiger Woods.

Think of your performance on each step as being like a dart-board that is split into six or eight pie-shaped slices, and has a num-ber of rings, each smaller than the one immediately to the outside of it. The bull's-eye, in the middle of the target, has the greatest scor-ing potential.

When you are playing darts, you throw your darts at the target, and the closer your dart strikes to the bull's-eye, the more points you score. If your dart strikes at the outermost ring, you score just a few points. But you do many times bet-ter if you hit the bull's-eye.

Now, every time you engage in one of the process steps, it's like throwing a dart at the target. You can hit the outer ring and score a few points, or hit closer to the bull's eye and score more. You can do each step of the process, or you can do each step bet-ter. And, like the ever-smaller rings of the target, there are de-grees of better. The bull's eye is always the vision of perfection.

As we discuss each step of the process, I'll show you how to do it, and then, how to do it better!

3

Finding the Right People

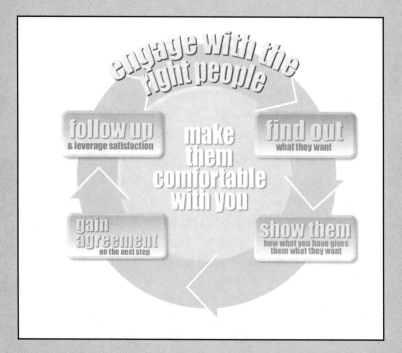

As we work through the sales process in each chapter, you'll find me saying that each step is critical. This one, however, is *really* critical. You may have the greatest product and the best price; you may be the most charismatic human being ever, with an extraordinary empathy for your customer, a persuasive presentation, and incredible closing skills. However, if you spend all your time with prospects who have no need for your product, no interest in it, no time to devote to you, and no money to spend, all of your superlative resources will be wasted.

On the other hand, if you have less-than-average sales skills and a mediocre product at a higher-than-market price, but you stumble across a prospect who desperately needs what you have, urgently wants to buy it, and has the money to spend, you are much more likely to make the sale and satisfy the customer.

Engaging the right people trumps every other piece of the sales process. If you can consistently do this well, you don't need to be exceptional at anything else. Your sales skills can be just adequate, but you'll be successful on the basis of your excellent execution of this key process step.

Of course, it's not that easily done. Many talented salespeople and valuable businesses have suffered through mediocre results because of their inability to do this well. It is, unfortunately, almost impossible to consistently and exclusively engage with the right people. A great deal of sales time is invested in just getting there. "Getting to the decision-maker" is an elusive but universal charge to every salesperson.

Engaging with the right people is the single-most important step you will take in your sales efforts.

This first and fundamental step in the process is composed of two sub-tasks that combine to make up this piece. As you'll see, for every piece of the puzzle, it is not enough that you do it, you must do it well!

Let's look at the two primary sub-tasks that combine in this crucial first step.

1. Decide who the right people are.
2. Find the best way to engage with them.

Decide Who the Right People Are

This is absolutely crucial work. The better you do this, the more likely you are to be successful.

Our natural tendency is to define the "right people" as broadly as possible, so as to include as many people as possible. When we take the opposite approach, however, we usually discover that it is a more powerful selling decision.

For example, one of my clients makes replacement parts for foreign cars. As long as he defined his market—the right people—as "owners of older foreign cars," he muddled along, unable to clearly identify the individuals within that general category, unable to create any visibility or credibility, and unable to distinguish himself from the multitudes of competitors.

Then he decided to narrow his focus. After a great deal of thought, he arrived at a much more clearly defined understanding of the "right people" for him: "Owners of two models produced by X manufacturer for the time period 1930 through 1980."

Armed with this narrow and precise definition of his market, he was able to create and deliver a catalogue followed by a Website that appealed to those people. He was able to find the media that appealed to them, and locate the shows and events they attended.

Then, because of the narrowness of the niche, he was able to dominate it, allowing him gross profits in the triple digits. Unless you are Pepsi Cola, Microsoft, or a Google, or someone who has hundreds of millions of dollars to spend on creating a marketing system that sells to everyone, you'll find that the more precise and specific you are in your definition, the easier it is to engage with those people.

That's our first rule: Precision and clarity are better than general and vague.

Precision and clarity are better than general and vague.

The decisions you make about the identity of "right people" are crucial to your success. Make the wrong decisions, and there is no overcoming it. Here is an example from a Website. A consultant friend was engaged in trying to identify why the site wasn't working, and I was asked to give my opinion. The site was extremely well done, and clearly a lot of money had been spent on the technical details. From a technical point of view, the site was possibly the best I'd ever seen.

However, the problem wasn't in the mechanics of the site. The site was designed to offer a product in which a large portion of the purchasing price would be donated to a series of causes. The buyer could stipulate which cause he wanted his money to go.

Here was the problem: There was no clear definition of who the right people were. For example, if you were someone who cultured a taste for that product, you wouldn't be interested in buying from this Website, because there were far more extensive selections and far higher-grade products readily available. If you were of the class of people who wanted to donate to some of the causes, you could do that directly, and get the tax write-off for it. So, who are the "right people?" People who didn't have much of a pallet for the product, didn't have much money to support the causes of their choice, and didn't mind paying considerably more for the product. Let's see. How many of those people are there?

The owner was guilty of the most common mistake made by start-up businesses: The entrepreneurs who start the business have an idea with which they become enamored. They are convinced of the power and appeal of that idea and put lots of time and effort into bringing it into fruition. However, they don't have a market for it. The world doesn't think nearly as much of the idea as the entrepreneur thinks of it. His great idea came to nothing because there weren't enough of the right people out there.

In this case, it was a Website and a business that probably absorbed hundreds of thousands of dollars. But it could just as well be the freelance professional trying to find someone to hire him, or the coffee shop that was located in the wrong place.

If you are an entrepreneur in a start-up mode, this is the most fundamental decision you can make. If you are a B2B salesperson, and you have never defined the precise group of "right people," you'll find yourself wasting hours and hours calling on people who just waste your time. Regardless of your unique circumstances, this decision trumps all the others.

> **The decision you make about who the "right people" are for you is the most fundamental sales decision.**

All the decisions that follow this one are dependent on it. If you are an entrepreneur starting a business, your definition of who the right people are will dictate the kind of business you start!

For example, if you want to start a Web-based business, but your "right people" are local and not very computer literate, you are probably destined for failure. If you are a professional hoping to freelance, and the people you define as the right people are a group of about 100 individuals within a 100 mile radius of your location, you would be stupid to invest in a Website.

You see, everything that follows—all the decisions you make as to how to appeal to them, what sort of offer is best, what medium is most effective, and so on, are all dependent upon this decision.

Here's an example: One of my clients represented a service that was particularly suited to trial lawyers. The decision to define the right people as trial lawyers within a certain geographical area then shaped and influenced the best way to engage with them, the kind of literature to create, the best words to use to approach them, etc. He discovered that one of his most effective prospecting strategies was to frequent the pubs where the trial lawyers often congregated at the end of the work day.

It is one thing if your "right people" are professional, and quite another if they are farmers. It is one thing if they are local, and quite another if they are spread out all over the country. It is one thing if you can look them up in the phone book, and quite another if they are protected by layers of gate-keepers.

Here's the point. All the decisions you make about how to sell are dependent on the decision about who you sell to.

> **All the decisions you make about how to sell are dependent on the decision as to who you sell to.**

Executing the Plan

Here is the question, the answer to which will do more to assure your success than any other single question: "Who is most likely to need/want what I have to offer?"

I know this sounds basic, but much of my career has been spent working with salespeople and sales organizations who have never really asked and answered that question. In order to come to a good decision, let's break that down into a number of smaller questions.

- Who needs or wants what you have?
- Who can pay for it?
- Are there enough of them to make it worth my time?
- How do I identify them?
- How can I gain access to them?

Who needs or wants what you have?

Describe the people or organizations that you think would need or want what you have. Remember, the more precisely you can describe them, the easier it is to sell to them.

Who can pay for what you have?

I hate to be so coarse, but the ultimate purpose of your sales effort is to get money. If the people who want it can't pay for it, you must adjust your sales strategy. For example, the world is full of college students who would love to have a new Corvette. However, only a small percentage of them can pay for it. So, if you are selling Corvettes, college students are not the right people. You'd be better off defining your "right people" as "50-ish, successful professional and business people."

Are there enough people to make it worth my time?

If there are only a handful of them, it's probably not a good business idea. I'm sure some of you were mentally arguing with my thinking in the previous paragraph. "Wait a minute," you thought, "there are some college students who could pay for a new Corvette." Probably so, but not enough of them to make it worth your time.

Think of the great Website effort described previously. How many pallet-less, penniless, gullible people are there? Not enough to make it worth your time. The answer to this question provides guidance as to how extensive your sales efforts can be. For example, if you're a freelancer looking for people to hire you to write grants, maybe 50 or so would be sufficient. If you are considering selling $5 homemade desserts over the internet, there had better be a whole lot more than 50 "right people." If there are five million "right people" you are going to need an entirely different sales approach than if there are 50 "right people."

How do I identify the right people?

Before you can engage with them, you have to identify who they are. The answer to this question requires you to move beyond the description of a group, say "50ish, successful business and professional people experiencing mid-life crises," to assessing the likelihood of you actually being able to populate that list with the names and contact information for the individuals within that group.

Do you know of a way to ferret out the individual organizations and/or people who populate your list? How accurate will your list be?

How can I gain access to them?

Remember: This is about engaging with the right people. First, we have to identify the right people and then we have to engage with them. If we know that we are not ever going to be able to engage with them, then they aren't the right people. The process is a bit circular, but effective, nonetheless.

Your definition of right people may be, for example, "former presidents of the United States." Unless you are really well-connected, or have the time, money, and energy to get really well-connected, you are just not going to ever gain access to them.

The Process

You can answer these questions broadly and generally, or you can answer them narrowly and specifically. Remember: Narrow and focused are better than broad and vague. However, you may have to begin with broad and vague and continually sharpen your focus by narrowing your answers. Do you recall the diagram of the dartboard from Chapter 2?

On a dartboard, the closer you get to the bull's-eye in the center, the more points you score. Each ring of the target, starting at the outer ring and working in, contains more and more potential for scoring. So it is with defining your right people. There are rings and layers of ways to define them.

Let me illustrate with my sales training practice as an example. I have great material for helping salespeople become better at selling. So, my larger universe of right people is the world of salespeople. Think of them as the outer-most ring.

However, not every salesperson is equal. We really do better with B2B salespeople than with others. So, although we have resources for every salesperson, we specialize in salespeople who operate within the B2B world. Let's label the next ring with that designation.

We can narrow this down even further. Within the world of B2B salespeople, I have a special affinity for wholesale distributors. So, let's draw another circle inside and label it "distributor salespeople."

Now, while salespeople are a market for us, and are the ultimate benefactors of what we do, they don't spend nearly as much money as their bosses spend. Thus, while a salesperson may spend $20 to buy a book from our Website, their boss has the ability to spend $20,000 to hire us to train all of his 20 salespeople. So, let's draw another circle inside and label it "sales leaders," understanding that it encompasses both sales managers and sales executives.

We are not done yet. A little experience leads us to the conclusion that not all sales leaders are equal. For example, although we have products and services that almost any principal can utilize, some have businesses that are too small to be lucrative targets for us. On the other hand, some of the folks in our potential market work in businesses that are too large—they have developed internal sales training programs, and have only limited interest in an outside source. So, let's apply that understanding to our target, and define the bull's-eye as "sales leaders in companies with annual sales volume of $20 million to $300 million."

We could keep going with this exercise in continually narrowing our focus until we reach a list of individual people, or, eventually, even one individual. In some selling situations, that's a good idea, but for now, let's stop there. We've defined several layers of "right people" starting with "salespeople" on the outer ring and progressively toward "sales leaders in distribution businesses that do between $20 and 300 million in annual sales."

As you can see there are layers of suitability for our definition of the right people.

> **There are layers of suitability for our definition of the right people.**

Let's now apply that concept to a number of possible scenarios. If you are in the initial stages of planning for a new business, you have a great opportunity to create a clear definition and build your business on that foundation. But you should do this exercise every year that you are in business. Things change. You gain more capabilities. The market changes. We teach B2B salespeople a process for determining the highest potential people within their sales territories annually. (See Chapter 4 of my book, 10 Secrets of Time Management for Salespeople)

So you are starting a coffee shop, and you have your eye on an empty spot at the strip mall down the street. When you start asking the question, "Who wants/needs what you have?" the first answer is: "People who like coffee." That's the outer ring.

Okay, but how can we filter through the world at large, and identify those who like coffee? Let's first narrow it down by geography. In all likelihood, people are not going to drive miles to buy your coffee, so you start by saying: "People who like coffee and live within a one mile radius of my shop." That's a more precise definition, and fills the next ring.

However, the strip mall is on a major thoroughfare, and just down the street is a large office complex with a lot of office workers. Let's account for them: "People who like coffee and live within a one mile radius of the shop, or who regularly drive by." That's the next ring toward the center.

Now we are stuck. So, let's think about ruling people out. Who would not be a possible candidate? I know you are thinking, "Well, anyone could like coffee." But some people are less likely than others. For this example let's say people under the age of 16 are probably not likely prospects, nor are people old than 70. Because you have a "luxury item," it probably won't be on the to-do list for parents of large families who need to spend their money on their children or household.

Let's incorporate all of that into our statement of who our "right people" are: "People who like coffee are between the ages of 17 and 70, are not parents of large families, and live within a one-mile radius of my shop or regularly drive by it."

We're getting closer to a precise definition of who the right people are for you. That may be as far as we can take it. In this case, that may be the bull's-eye.

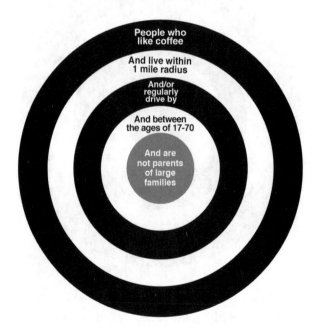

Let's apply the same process and principles to another scenario. You are an unemployed professional who has decided to establish a freelance practice. You were employed as a design consultant in a private consulting firm, and you have some expertise in writing grant applications. So, you decide to freelance as a grant application writer.

Who needs your service? You can start with "non-profit organizations looking for money." That's the outer ring. However, not all of them will need your business. Some of the larger organizations probably have internal staff to do that. You want organizations that are too small to have a full-time dedicated staff person do it, but not so small that they can't pay for the service.

Let's say that you use those guidelines to narrow down your definition to this: "Non-profit organizations with annual budgets between $200,000 and $5 Million." That's the next ring.

But, organizations don't make decisions, people do. So, let's narrow it down even more for the next ring: "Executive directors of non-profit organizations with annual budgets between $200,000 and $5 million."

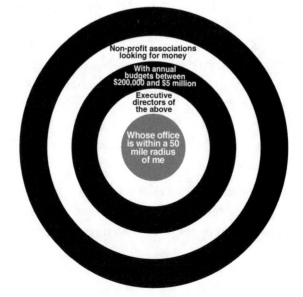

Let's now take geography into mind and add another, deeper layer:

"Whose office is within a 50 mile radius of me."

Your quest to precisely define the set of right people could continue on for several more layers. You could, for example, narrow it down by type of non-profit, or, to add some urgency, those who just had their government grant money reduced.

You get the idea. This process and set of principles, applied to any selling situation, any where, with any medium, will, more than any other single decision, determine the relative success of that selling effort.

And, its application is far more extensive than just at the beginning of a new venture. For existing businesses, the issue is more likely one of degree than initial definition. In other words, you already have customers. The issue is what types of customers are more right than others?

For example, I'll frequently work with a group of salespeople who spend much of their time calling on the wrong people—sometimes for years. They invest their selling time in those customers with whom they get along and for whom they feel some affinity, and who can be counted on to see and interact with them. Often, those customers are on the outer rings of their target—the C and D customers. They can buy, but they are not as lucrative as those closer to the bull's-eye—the A and B customers.

If you are wondering what is wrong with you the answer is that it is the wrong set of criteria. They should be defining the right people as those who have greater potential and philosophies and values that compliment their company's philosophies and values. Because they never really thought it through, they wallow in mediocre performance, sometimes for their entire careers, hindered by the lack of a clear, precise definition of who the right people really are.

As they spend more and more of their time with the customers closer to the bull's-eye, and less time with those on the outer fringes, they become increasingly more effective.

If you have an existing sales effort, then the questions you should ask and answer have slightly different wording to them. The basic question is this:

"With which customers is my time most effectively invested?"

Your task is to define the bull's-eye, and then to invest your sales resources as close to the bull's-eye as possible. In order to do that, you ought to examine your prospect and customer list and ask:

- Who needs or wants what I have the most? (How big is the opportunity?)
- Who is most able to pay for it? (Who is financially solvent?)
- Who is most compatible with my company and me?

Methodically going through this process annually will keep you focused on the highest potential customers and, more than anything else, positively impact your sales success.

Find Someone Else to Help You

This is one of those tasks where two heads are always better than one. Because the answers you come up with are so crucial to your success, you want to make sure that the answers are the best and most accurate they can be.

That is particularly true for this exercise. You are generally too close to the situation to see it clearly. Your vision will be clouded by your emotional attachment to your idea. So, bring in someone else to help you. If you are a freelance professional or business that means you should bring in someone with successful sales and/or business experience who does not have a vested interest in the idea and have him or her review your work and challenge your answers.

If you are an established salesperson or sales executive, that means bringing in a consultant or someone credible from outside your company to provide those fresh, objective eyes to your answers.

Engaging With the Right People

Okay, we've gotten a great understanding of how important it is to define the right people, and we have a sense of how to do that. We're halfway through the first step. Remember, the first step of our sales process is to "engage with the right people." First we have to define who they are; that's the "right people" piece, and then we have to interact with them; that's the "engage" piece.

The Encarta Dictionary definition of "engage" is: "To involve somebody in an activity." That's a good starting point. Before they can buy from you, they must become involved with you.

> **Before they can buy from you,**
> **they must become involved with you.**

That involvement can be very superficial, as in 45 to 60 seconds of roaming around your Website, to very intense, as in a 20-year relationship between a B2B buyer and seller.

Regardless of *the level* of involvement, it must be characterized by three components: Attention, Interest, and Action.

You must attract the prospect's attention, you must gain some degree of their interest, and you must motivate them to take some action.

Now, let's put these concepts together and see how they play out in a couple scenarios.

You are starting that coffee shop in the strip mall. You've defined the right people as the people who drive by on their way to work. So, how can you "engage" with them? You think "Attention, Interest, Action." Step one: Get their attention. Because they are driving by the strip mall every day, you decide that a portable sign with a flashing light will do the trick. Now, however, you must get their interest. Again, because they are on their way to work, you decide to spin off that common interest they all have and put these words on your sign: "Start Work Sharp! Hot Coffee Special!" Underneath that you put the words "Turn Right Now" with a big right turn arrow.

When someone brakes and turns right, you've accomplished this step. You haven't sold them anything, but you've engaged them. You gained their attention, captured their interest, and prompted them to take action. You are on your way.

Here's another example.

Let's say you are that freelance professional trying to find short-term projects writing grant proposals. You've narrowed the world of "right people" down to 100 relatively local non-profit organizations. You've done a lot of homework, and doggedly uncovered the names of the key decision-makers in those organizations. Now you need to engage them.

So you consider your options. You could send them each an e-mail. That might get through to a couple of them, but probably will be ignored by almost all of them. You could call, but you would probably get voice mail, leave a message and never hear back from them. You could write a letter. The chances of that getting through are a bit greater than the e-mail, but still the chances are not great. Or, you could just show up, and hope to see them. That might make you look desperate.

After a lot of thought, you decide to create a one-page case study—a description of a grant you successfully obtained for one of your previous employers, and complete with full color, pictures of the former employer, the amount of the check, and maybe a positive comment from the former employer. Then, you write a one-page letter of introduction, and mail the package special delivery, signature required, five a day for 20 days. On the day that the package is delivered, you call and leave a voice-mail message, referencing the package and asking for a few minutes on the phone.

It's a lot of work, but these 100 people hold your livelihood in their hands. It is worth it. Should it work and create some attention and interest, they may even return your voice mail and make the appointment. In that case, great! They have taken some action, and you have them engaged! You haven't gotten a project, but you've made it through the first step of the process. You are one step closer.

Let's reflect on this discussion of a couple of widely different sales situations and widely different solutions to the problem of engaging the prospect. One conclusion we can come to is this: There are a variety of different ways of engaging the prospect, and they vary in intensity.

There are a variety of different ways of engaging the prospect, and they vary in intensity.

Think of a spectrum upon which every possible level of interaction is mapped. On the left side of the spectrum is the least intense involvement you can think of, and on the right end is the most intense.

Our two examples approach both ends of the spectrum.

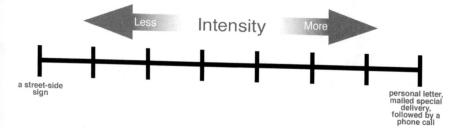

That observation should lead to a question: How intense should my effort to engage the customer be?

The answer lies in the mix of several variables. For example, generally speaking, the more customers you need, the less intense your engagement strategy. In your coffee shop, for example, you may need a couple thousand customers to make you profitable. For the freelancer, two or three will do the trick.

Here's another one: Generally speaking, the larger the dollar volume of the purchase, the more intense the engagement strategy. Using our two examples, you really can't afford to write a letter and follow up with a phone call for a $3 latte, but you could for a $30,000 project.

The state of the competition is another factor. If there are a bunch of options out there for the prospect, you'll need to be especially clever to penetrate the cloud of competing choruses and grab his attention. If there are few, you won't need to invest so much money and time in this step of the process.

The history the customer has with you and your company is another important variable. The world is full of B2B salespeople who can merely call a customer on the phone and say, "I'm going to be in town next week, and would like to get together with you." Because the customer has an on-going relationship with the company and salesperson, the phone call is all that is usually necessary to engage with the customer.

Let's go back to our two examples and extract another lesson. As we think about both situations, the question naturally arises: What if they don't work? Good question. Common sense leads us to the answer: If the engagement strategies don't work, then they'll have to try something else.

Our coffee shop, for example, could be disappointed in the number of cars willing to make that sharp right turn into the strip mall and instead decide to print out coupons, offer a dollar off on the first latte, and distribute them to everyone in the offices down the road.

Our freelance consultant may only get a half-hearted response from one voice mail after all that work. Next step? Maybe show up at their office, and ask the secretary to request a five minute face-to-face meeting with the person in charge.

Rarely does one engagement strategy work for everyone, and rarely does it work forever. So, if you want to be successful in any large measure, you'll need to create multiple engagement strategies, and review and refine them constantly.

> **Create multiple engagement strategies, and review and refine them constantly.**

In my business, for example, when we have an event we want our customers to attend, we use all means of communication. We mail first-class snail mail letters (sometimes we send them special delivery). We send e-mails. We advertise in our Ezine and on our Website. We advertise in newsletters and journals that serve our markets. We call them on the phone. No one thing works for everyone in our market. So, we choose to use a full variety of methods to reach our market.

Of course, the strategies to engage the prospect are limitless. This is a place where creativity can make all the difference. Here are two great examples of creative approaches to this step in the process.

One of my clients was an advertising agency. They had identified 100 "right people"—the key people in their market and location who held the future of the advertising agency in their hands. They had accomplished the first step—identifying the right people—with excellence.

Now, the problem was to move them to interact with the agency. The experienced team knew that those key people with whom they needed to interact were busy and difficult people to see. They just wouldn't respond to the normal channels. So, they came up with this very creative way of engaging with their prospects.

They sent each of the 100 prospects a box, about the size of a watch box. It was wrapped in brown paper and contained no return address. The name and address of the prospect was hand-written in female handwriting. Inside the box was a sugar cube and a small piece of paper, like the size of a fortune cookie message, with the words, "Keep it sweet."

That was it. Nothing else.

One week later, those same prospects were sent another box, wrapped and addressed in exactly the same fashion. This time, it contained a lemon with the message, "Don't let it go sour."

Again, nothing else in the box.

On the third week, yet another box, wrapped and packaged identically. This time, the box contained tinsel, like what you use to decorate a Christmas tree. The message? "Make it sparkle."

Once again, nothing else.

Week four and yet one more box arrived, identical to the others. This time there was only one thing inside—a business card from the advertising agency salesperson, with a self-stick note stuck to it. On the note was the hand-written message, "I'll call you tomorrow for an appointment."

Of the 100 people who received that series of deliveries, every single one of them took the call and made the appointment. The advertising agency, when faced with the difficult task of engaging the prospect, had developed an effective and creative solution. They gained their prospect's attention, they captured their interest, and they prompted them to take action—they took the phone call and made the appointment. In other words, they engaged the right people!

> **The more competing demands there are on for the prospect, the more creative you must be to penetrate through the blizzard and have your message recognized.**

It doesn't take much thought to realize that there are a virtually unlimited number of choices when it comes to engaging the customer. Here's a review of some of them. Let's use our spectrum from the least intense to the very intense as a way of organizing them.

Starting on the left for a retail operation, it begins with the company's location, signage, and store front. Are they inviting, do they attract the prospect's interest, and do they prompt them to come in?

If those are sufficient, good for you. If not, then you need to advertise—to reach out in the world of apathy and ignorance and attract people into your establishment. Now the focus shifts to your advertising. Are you reaching the right people? Are you attracting them, interesting them, prompting them to come into your place in sufficient quantity? There are literally dozens of books written on this subject.

But traditional advertising is a relatively non-intense method, in that it only addresses the senses of sight and sound, and the prospect can be totally passive. Picture yourself in front of the TV, scanning a Website, or listening to the radio on the way to work.

If you can add scent to the mix, you'll be more intense, and more likely to gain the prospect's attention. Think of the bakeries, candle shops, and ethnic restaurants of the world, some of which have fans positioned to blow the aromas out into the mall and entice people inside.

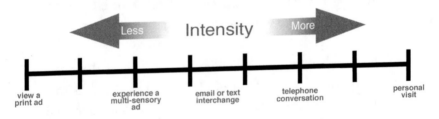

Engaging a prospect through a conversation is more intense. If you can get them in a conversation on the phone, for example, you'll engage more people than if you just send them a post card. In this case, your tone of voice, your cadence, and the actual words that you say are all elements of your effort to engage them, and should be carefully considered and mindfully chosen.

If you show up at their office in person and engage them in a conversation, you'll have even better results. Now, your appearance is important and in play. How you are dressed, your posture, body language, hair cut, and so on, are all elements of that first moment, and they impact the prospect's decision as to whether or not they should engage with you. That quickly morphs into your actions: your smile, hand shake, and eye contact, as well as your conversation including your tone of voice, dialect, and choice of words—all these impact the prospect and affect your ability to engage with them. As in every process in this book, the way you come to the final outcome is to ask yourself the right questions, in the right sequence, and write the answers down with as much detail as possible.

1. How many prospects do you need to engage, and how frequently do you need to engage them?

If you are the freelance grant writer, maybe 10 will do it. If you are developing the coffee shop, maybe a couple of hundred a day, every day. If you are creating an Ecommerce Website, you may need a few thousand every day.

2. What resources do you have to apply to the task?

This includes money, of course. But you may also have other resources, such as connections with people, locations, partnerships, and so on. The answer to this question puts the limits on your efforts and, in so doing, helps define and inform your decision. For example, if you have $1,000 to spend, you may be able to create some signage that will bring people into your coffee shop. You will probably not, however, be able to create a system that will drive thousands of people a day to your Website.

3. What about your "right people"?

Where are they, can you identify them, where do they go now, who knows them, how can you reach them, and what media are they currently engaged with?

Here we are again with the often-repeated cliché of "knowing your market." The more you know about the right people, the easier it is to decide how to engage them. Think of the thousands of people driving by the strip mall, versus the 100 key prospects for our freelancer.

This is such a powerful step in the process that it is not unusual to think of ideas as to the best way to engage them.

4. What is it about your product/Website/service that would be of interest and benefit to your group of "right people"?

Ultimately, you are bringing something to your right people that you hope they will buy. In a world of others like you, why should they buy what you have? What is there about your offer that would be of interest to them?

This may be the most important question to ask, as it speaks to the heart of your effort to sell something. It may seem elementary, but I have seen countless business owners, VPs of sales, and salespeople who, when confronted with the question, were stunned and speechless.

One of the services that my company offers is a week-long, intense sales training session. We have two trainers work with six salespeople from 8 a.m. to 5 p.m. for five days. Every day, they role-play a situation, have it video recorded, play it back, and have it critiqued, and then do it again better the next time.

You can imagine that this is an intimidating experience for the trainees. Typically, because of the expense, it is limited to experienced salespeople.

On Monday morning, in order to ease the tension, I ask people to just talk about their first role-play—introducing themselves to a prospect in a cold call. In order to get them thinking about it, I ask them to tell me why someone would do business with them. The overwhelming response to the question, "Why would I do business with you?" is silence. For the most part, they don't know. They have never thought about it.

Don't put yourself in their shoes. Formulate a powerful and specific answer to the question, "Why should someone buy it?"

As you compile the answers to these questions, you'll probably have lots of ideas pop into your head. If not, then look carefully at your answers and consider this: *What is the most effective way of engaging the quantity of prospects that I'll need to be successful, given my market, my message, and my means?*

You are probably not going to come up with the perfect solution with your first attempt. And, even if you do, it won't last forever. Things change and so does your market. So, on a regular basis, you'll need to examine and improve your efforts.

In order to do that, you'll need to measure the effectiveness of your efforts. At this stage of the sales process, that's pretty easy. All you need to do is count the number of people you engage in a specific time frame.

Remember, you are engaged in a process. Six simple steps. But for the end result to be what you want it to be, each step of the process should be done as well as you can do it. So, it's not enough to measure only the end result—how much you sold today—you must measure each step along the way.

So, back to our coffee shop. The question is: How many people came in this week? You'll worry about how much they bought later, but for now, we just want to keep track of the first step of the process. So, you measure the number of bodies that walk through the door. High tech: install a sensor. Low tech: hire a teenager to count them.

For our freelancer, telemarketer, or any B2B salesperson for that matter, the question is, "How many of the right people talked with me on the phone?" You can use a simple form and just make a hash mark for each person.

For the Website, you can be even more precise. For the question, "How many people did we attract and interest? The answer is "the number of unique visitors to your site." When we add the third part, "How many people did we attract, interest, and spur to some action?" the answer is in the bounce rate on the index page.

At some point you will have a number. That is the measurement of effectiveness of your engagement strategy. Let's do one more thing with it: Let's figure out how much each one of those cost us. Just add up the total cost of your engagement strategy and divide it by the number of people you engaged.

Back to our coffee shop example. What were the costs?

1. Your labor. It took you about eight hours to come up with the words, to arrange for the sign, to

create the message on the sign, and so on. You figure your time is worth maybe $25 an hour, so your labor was $200.

2. The sign. It cost you $500 to rent it for the month and $50 in electricity to power it. So, we add in $550 and get $750.

That's pretty simple. So we take the $750 and divide it by 600—the number of people who came into the coffee shop during its first month. We get a cost per engaged prospect of $1.25. Oops. If the average sale is $2.25, netting you a gross profit of $1 each, you are losing money on every one.

At this point, we have two measurements. The first measurement is what I call the "measure of effectiveness." It basically answers the question, "How well is this effort doing what I want it to do?" If, for example, you wanted to attract 500 people into your coffee shop, then your approach is very effective. It's actually doing more than you expected it to do.

The second measure, the dollar average, is what I call efficiency. It basically answers the question, "To what degree is it costing us an appropriate amount?" In our example the answer is, "Not at all."

Any combination of those two is possible. For example, your effort can be:

■   Effective, but not efficient.
■   Effective and efficient.
■   Not effective and efficient.
■   Not effective and not efficient.

Each of these leads us to a course of inquiry and action that ultimately is designed to remedy the situation and do it better.

If our analysis shows that our effort is "effective, but not efficient," as is the case with our coffee shop, the answer probably lies in finding ways to reduce the cost. Maybe a smaller sign is the answer?

If we discover that our engagement strategy is sufficiently "effective and efficient," then we're best advised to leave it alone, and measure it again in a few months.

If we discover that it is "not effective and efficient," then we probably should go back to the drawing board, and brainstorm some completely different approach.

And if we find that it is "not effective and not efficient," it may very well be that our fundamental offering, "coffee in this location," is flawed. Redo the whole strategy, or question whether you should be in this business.

The most likely result of your numbers analysis will probably not be quite so absolute as the previous numbers indicated. Probably, you'll see that you could be a little bit more effective, or a little bit more efficient. In those cases, you tweak the message and the medium and measure the impact of your efforts the next month.

This is one of the reasons why most small businesses fail in the first year. They just didn't have enough time and money to get it right.

Start right away with measuring and refining. Make it a regular discipline. Every week, or every month, measure your results and refine your efforts, understanding that you will never be perfect, or even finished. It's a process. That's how you do it better.

Every week, or every month, measure your results and refine your efforts, understanding that you will never be perfect, or even finished. It's a process.

Note: We have assembled a variety of resources to help you with this step of the process. Visit *http://www.sellanythingtoanyone. net/engage.php* to review them.

How to Implement the Ideas in This Chapter

1. Review these principles:
    - This is the single biggest decision you will make in your sales efforts.
    - Precision and clarity are better than general and vague.
    - The decisions you make about who the "right people" are for you are the most fundamental sales decisions.
    - All the decisions you make as to how to sell are dependent on the decision as to who your customers are going to be.
    - There are layers of suitability for your definition of the right people.

2. If you are starting your sales effort, ask and answer the following questions, in writing, and in ever more specific detail.
    - Who needs or wants what I have the most?
    - Who can pay for it?
    - Are there enough of them to make it worth my time?
    - Can I identify them?
    - How can I get to them?

3. If you are in an existing sales effort, then ask the questions with a slightly different focus:
   - Who needs or wants what I have the most? (How big is the opportunity?)
   - Who is most able to pay for it?
   - Who is most compatible with my company and me?

4. Find someone else to help you with this.

5. Before they can buy from you, they must become involved with you.

6. There are a variety of different ways of engaging the prospect, and they vary in intensity.

7. Create multiple engagement strategies, and review and refine them constantly.

8. The more competing demands there are on the time of the prospect, the more creative you must be to penetrate through the blizzard and have your message recognized.

9. Answer the following questions:
   - How many prospects do you need to engage, and how frequently do you need to engage them?
   - What resources do you have to apply to the task?
   - What do you know about your "right people?"
   - What is there about your solution/store/service/product/Website that would be of benefit to your group of right people? Why would they be interested in what you have?

10. Every week, or every month, measure your results and refine your efforts, understanding that you will never be perfect, or even finished.

4

Making the Customer Comfortable With You

Imagine two gears grinding together. Apply some lubrication at the point at which they touch. As a result, the heat from the friction is dissipated and the gears work more smoothly. If you were to stop lubricating the gears, sooner or later they would break down and stop working. Clearly, where two independent pieces of steel rub together in regular interaction, lubrication is necessary to make everything work well.

The sales process is much like that. Think of you and your customer as those two independent gears, regularly interacting. Where two people (you and your prospect) interact, it sure helps to apply some oil into the gears. That oil is composed of certain thoughts and feelings we generate in the prospect. Simply put, we must make them comfortable with us. We must create some rapport, and appear to be credible.

Notice in our diagram the area labeled as "Make them comfortable with you" is not a step in the process, but rather it fills all the space between the steps, and touches every step. That is to convey the idea that making them comfortable with you does not have a beginning and ending, but rather it is something you do from the very first moment the prospect encounters you, in every interaction along the way, until the very last moment the customer goes on his way. The need to make them comfortable with you influences everything you do.

> **The need to make them comfortable with you influences everything you do.**

Is it essential? Pretty much. It is possible for a transaction to take place when the buyer isn't comfortable with the seller, but it is much more difficult for both parties, and usually only happens when the buyer feels he has no other options. As soon as the buyer feels like he has some other option, he'll move on.

From your perspective, trying to sell something without making the customer feel comfortable with you is like swimming against the current. You can do it for awhile at a great cost of time and energy, but you are ultimately going to be worn out and defeated.

So what, exactly, does it mean to "make the prospect comfortable with you"?

At the least, it means they must believe you and/or your organization to be *capable* and *credible*. At the most it means that you must create and sustain a relationship with the customer in which they must *know* you and your organization well, *trust* you, and believe that you *understand* and *relate* to them.

Before we define these terms, let's note a couple of principles. First, as you look at the previous paragraph you should notice that every piece of the definition of what it means to be comfortable with you takes place in the mind or heart of the prospect. In other words, the definition of your success at this essential skill is what the customer thinks and feels about you. I tell salespeople all the time, "The relationship is 100 percent defined by the customer."

The relationship is 100 percent defined by the customer.

What the customer thinks and feels about you is all that counts. To be successful at this, beginning with the first impression and extending through every contact, communication, and transaction, you must focus on the thoughts and feelings your decisions and actions have on the customer.

Second, there is a direct relationship between the amount of risk your customer must assume when he buys from you and the degree to which you must make him comfortable. If, for example, you want him to buy a $10 CD on your Website, you don't have to dramatically impact his feelings about you. On the other hand, if you are selling a $500,000 piece of production equipment, or asking the customer to invest his life savings with you, he sure better have a relationship with you before you ask him to make that decision.

What Is Risk?

Risk is several things. Risk is the combination of the financial, social, emotional, and time costs that the company and the individual decision-maker will bear as a result of making a mistake.

Risk is the answer to these two questions:

1. "What happens to my company if I make the wrong decision?"
2. "What happens to me if I make the wrong decision?"

Risk is often the number-one issue in the mind of the customer, particularly when that customer has no history with you or your company. That makes it the number one issue to address in the sales process.

Risk is what the customer perceives it to be. In other words, it's not anything quantifiable, such as the price of your offer. It's not objective or tangible. Instead, it is much more insidious, lurking underneath almost every decision the customer makes. In fact, most customers are not even aware of the idea of risk. They just know what they feel and fear.

Because risk rises out of fear, risk is often not mentioned. To acknowledge risk is to admit fear. To admit fear is, in many people's minds, to expose weaknesses. No one wants to look weak.

> **Risk is the combination of the financial, social, emotional, and time costs that the company and the individual decision-maker will bear as a result of making a mistake.**

In my seminars I help people understand risk with these two examples. Let's say that on the way home tonight, your spouse calls you on the cell phone and explains that some friends are coming over for the evening. You need to stop at the grocery store on the way home and pick up some disposable cups so that you'll have something in which to serve the drinks.

You stop at the grocery store, rush in and see brand A and brand B. You select brand B, scoot through the express lane, and arrive home just a few moments before your guests are scheduled to arrive. Your spouse has a pitcher of margaritas, and you pour yourself one in the disposable cup you just bought. As you raise it to your lips to take a sip, you discover a leak in the bottom. You quickly grab another cup, pour the contents of the defective cup into that one, and raise it to your mouth. Oops! A leak in that one, too. One after the other, you discover that every one of the cups you bought is defective. What price are you paying for your mistake?

I don't know about you, but in my house I'd be the recipient of some negative emotion from my spouse. There would be a social and emotional price to pay. I'd also have to invest additional time running back to the store to fix the problem with another bag of disposable cups. I'd have to pay for them, so there would be some additional financial costs.

Imagine all of this fuss over a simple little purchase. Even so, when you compare the risk of this decision with all possible decisions you could make in your life, this one has relatively little risk. Here's a simple exercise to help you understand this concept. Notice the following diagram. Assume it is a measurement of the risk involved with every possible decision you can make. Very risky decisions are closer to the 100, and decisions of small risk are near the zero.

Now on this scale of zero to 100, where would you put the risk of buying a package of disposable cups? It's close to zero.

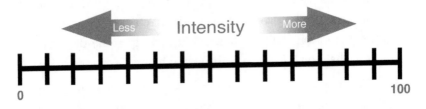

Next, let's compare that with a risk on the other end of the equation. For a number of years, I had an international adoption agency as a client. Consider a young lady in a crisis pregnancy. What is the risk involved as she contemplates signing up her unborn child to adoption? Certainly a lifetime of consequences for at least four people. On our zero-to-100 scale, most people would rate it as a 100. This risk is at the opposite end of the spectrum.

The point here is that different decisions carry with them different degrees of risk. Now, put yourself in the shoes of the individual who is making the decision to buy your products. What happens to that person if he or she makes a mistake?

Now I know you are thinking that you and your company will make it right, so that there really is no risk. But that's your perspective, not your customer's. He doesn't know that you'll make things right. Even if you say it, he still doesn't necessarily believe it. So, put yourself in his shoes and see the situation through his eyes. On the zero-to-100 scale, how much risk does he accept when he says yes to you? Here's an easy way of calculating it. Just ask yourself what happens to that individual if you, or your company, mess up.

Hopefully, you now have a different perspective on that prospective customer who is attracted to your pricing. It's not about the price, it's not about the quality, and it's not about the service, it's all about the risk!

This understanding of risk is crucial to your success. Remember, sales is all about helping the customer make a decision, and the biggest underlying issue in the customer is the risk.

Every decision the customer makes carries with it some degree of risk. The greater the perception of risk, the greater the relationship must be (the degree to which they become comfortable with you) in order to enable them to take the risk.

The greater the perception of risk, the greater must be the relationship must be (the degree to which they become comfortable with you) in order to enable them to take the risk.

Let's use our now familiar tool of a spectrum from one extreme to the other to illustrate this concept. Here's our spectrum again, upon which we can place every possible decision that a prospect makes in deciding to buy from you. To keep it simple, let's illustrate using products/services for an individual.

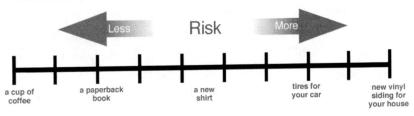

As we go from the far left to the far right, the risk increases. So, if you buy a book from an online Website and it comes to you damaged and not what you wanted, you may be out some time trying to get it fixed, or you may just chalk it up to experience and move on. Maybe the total impact is a few minutes and $10. On the other end of the spectrum, if you hire someone to install new vinyl siding on your home and the color is off, the workmanship poor, and it starts to buckle and crack within a few months, you've got a major issue on your hands. You've reduced the value of your home, increased your stress level, squandered hours trying to get some satisfaction, and maybe threw away thousands of dollars on a bad decision.

Now let's create a parallel spectrum, this one laying out the depth and degree to which you must make the customer feel comfortable with you in order to enable him to buy.

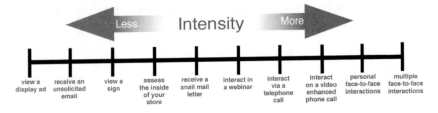

At the far left are relatively non-intense efforts. If your Website looks like it works, has a responsive Ecommerce function, and shows a picture of the book you want to buy, that's probably enough capability and credibility to make you feel comfortable with the risk.

If your coffee shop looks relatively inviting, no one is writhing on the floor with intestinal cramps, the coffee smells good, and the waiters understand English, that's probably enough capability and credibility to make you feel comfortable in ordering a $3 latte.

None of those, however, would be sufficient to make you comfortable with signing a contract for a $15,000 vinyl siding job and writing a check for a good portion of that up front. You are not going to order that over the Web.

You'll probably want to meet the salesperson face-to-face, review his literature, check out some of his former customers, and so on. As the risk increases for the customer, the need for you to make him or her feel comfortable with you increases proportionately.

The same principles can be applied to business-to-business selling. For example, if you are selling a package of paper hand towels to the maintenance supervisor of a manufacturing company, that carries with it a minimal degree of risk. If, however, you are selling a piece of production equipment to the plant manager, the risk of a mistake with that purchase is huge.

The decision that you make to accurately assess how much risk the customer accepts when he or she says yes to you is one of the bedrock, fundamental decisions that will inform everything you do. If your offer is on the left side of the spectrum, then you can use relatively non-intense means of making them comfortable.

If, however, your offer is positioned on the right side of the spectrum, you must go beyond just the initial perceptions of capability and credibility, and create and sustain a relationship with the customer in which they must *know* you and your organization well, *trust* you, and believe that you *understand* and *relate* to them.

It's a considerably more intense, much more complex, and more expensive challenge.

A number of years ago, I was approached by a young man who was the VP of Sales for a new company. He had a state-of-the-art, hot new product, but was having difficulty selling it. Since then, the product has become something of a commodity, but at the time, it was on the leading edge of technology. These computerized controls were retro-fit onto food processing machinery, dramatically reducing the amount of energy the equipment used, and paying for themselves within six to eight months of reduced energy bills.

Sounded like a good idea.

However, he was having trouble selling them. "Tell me how you sell them," I asked. He described his way of identifying the right people—plant managers in food-processing plants. Then he explained that he called and got the plant manager on the phone and collected information as to the number and types of equipment. He would then create a written proposal, send it to the prospect, and follow up with a phone call to ask for the order.

"I think the problem is I have too much fluff in the proposal," he said. "I need to cut right to the dollars and cents impact."

"Let me see if I have this right," I said. "You are in your late 20s right?"

"Yes."

"And your prospects are senior managers who are probably twice your age, probably with advanced degrees, and maybe 10 to 15 years tenure in that plant?"

"Yeah, probably."

"So, you are asking someone twice your age, with far more education, to risk his job and spend $40,000 to $60,000 on a product he has never seen, a company he has never heard of, and a person he has never met. Is that right?"

"Well, if you put it that way," he said.

"Put it that way," I said, "because that is how your customer sees it. It is not about 'fluff' in the proposal; it is about a lack of a relationship sufficient to warrant the prospect taking the risk you are asking him to take."

The solution in this case was to create some marketing collateral to create credibility, and to define a sales process that included five face-to-face visits before we asked the customer to take the risk.

You see, the amount of risk that you ask the customer to take determines the level of the relationship you must build with him before asking him to take that risk.

The amount of risk that you ask the customer to take determines the level of the relationship you must build with him before asking him to take that risk.

Now that you've gained an understanding of how crucial this is, let's go back and drill a bit deeper into what it really means to "make them comfortable with you."

At the far left end of the spectrum in relatively low-risk decisions, you just need to convey the idea that you and your company are *capable* and *credible*. *Capable* means that you convey the idea to your prospect that you are able to do what you claim you can do. This can be very simple.

In our coffee shop example, when someone walks in and notices the coffee urns and the coffee cups, smells brewing coffee in the air, and sees your wait staff serving coffee, that is going to be sufficient to convey the idea that you are capable of delivering a hot cup of coffee.

Credible means they believe your claims are convincing and trustworthy.

So, when your sign says, "Organic, Costa Rican coffee," they believe that.

At this level, the process is a matter of common sense. You just look at your offering from the perspective of a prospect encountering it for the first time and ask, "Does it look and feel like we are capable and credible?" Focus on the first impression of your store, your Website, or whatever your vehicle is for selling.

Pay attention to the details. People judge your capability at the big things by your proficiency at the little things. This lesson was brought home to me in a dramatic way a number of years ago. For some reason, I fished a crumpled-up letter out of the waste basket. This was a marketing letter we had sent to a list of prospects. The letter contained two typos.

One of the prospects circled the typos and wrote across the top of the letter, "If you can't spell correctly, how good can you be at marketing?" He sent it back to us, and my marketing assistant—the person responsible for the letter—had wadded it up and thrown it away, hoping that I wouldn't see it. But I did. She was fired and we instituted a policy that says, "Nothing goes out of the office without someone else proofing it."

If you have a typo on your Website or e-mail solicitations, for example, you will lose customers who see you as incompetent. If your coffee shop is dirty, the tables not promptly bussed and old newspapers scattered randomly about, you will appear less than capable. When it comes to conveying the impression of your credibility and capability, the devil truly is in the details.

As is almost always the case, you may be too close to your efforts to see them from the perspective of a customer. Ask someone else to critique your offer from a "credible and comfortable" perspective.

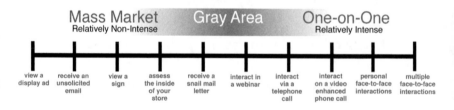

Let's return to the spectrum. Notice that we are breaking our "comfort/relationship" spectrum down into three separate stages. On the far left are the relatively non-intense relationships like the one we just described. Let's call those "mass market." These sales situations are characterized by a large quantity of relatively low-risk decisions, made by a relatively large quantity of customers. A Website selling books or CDs is an example of this type of sales situation, as is the coffee shop we've been discussing.

On the far right are the much more intense, higher-risk decisions that require a positive business relationship with a person and a company. The grant writer is an example of this sales situation, as are investment managers and most B2B companies. Let's call this class of selling situation "one-on-one." In this class, the prospect must feel like he or she has a relationship with the individual representing the selling organization, as well as with the organization itself, in order to feel comfortable enough to make a high-risk decision.

Notice that there is a gray area in between, where the two different approaches overlap. In this area, both the risk and the need for relationships are somewhere between the two extremes. If your mass market efforts are *really good,* you can motivate these people to do business with you. It is a whole lot easier, though, if they feel like they know you. Unfortunately, from your point of view, there is generally not enough money in it to warrant you being personally involved.

Here's a simple illustration. Let's say you become thirsty on a drive to your grandmother's house. You pull into a service station and see that they have a convenience store. It looks clean and organized. You walk in, find the cooler, and see three different sizes and brands of water. You pick one on the basis of its size, label, and price, and off you go.

That's the mass market selling situation. From the seller's perspective, the label, the price, the cooler, the store, and the signage all combined to make you comfortable with that purchase.

Now, let's say you are in the business of bottling that water and selling it.

You want to build a new bottling plant and you are applying to the bank for a loan of $1,000,000 to finance the new plant. You are deeply into the realm of the one-on-one relationship. That banker is going to want to see you, and personally talk with you, as well as examine your plans, your history, and your character before he is going to give you $1,000,000.

What about the gray area in between? You realize after you bought a case of water that your refrigerator is broken and you must replace it. You are probably not going to buy one online. You'll probably want to see it, talk with the person who is selling it, and gain a sense of the credibility and capability both of the brand, as well as the local seller before you write a check for $1,000. You don't need to have a relationship, but you do want to feel good about the people and organization on the other side of this transaction.

One of the issues here is your marketing communications; the mode of communication you choose to use has a direct impact on the customer's feeling about you.

For example, a display ad in the local newspaper will rarely generate intense feelings, nor will an unsolicited e-mail. A snail mail letter will be a bit more personal and interactive. A photo of a real person, sent with that letter, will establish a bit more of a relationship. A telephone call or Webinar will create a bit more of a relationship. A video-enhanced telephone call will be better yet. And an interaction with a live human being is the most intense of all of these.

Do you see the pattern? The more your techniques and communications involve interactions with real people, the greater is the degree of relationship (oil in the gears) you build with the customer. The greater the relationship you develop, the greater the risk the customer is willing to take.

To be good at this, you accurately match your "oil the gears" decisions to the risk for the customer.

Note: We have assembled a variety of resources to help you accomplish this step of the process. Visit *http://www.sellanythingtoanyone.net/comfortable.php* to review them.

How to Implement the Ideas in This Chapter

1.   Decide where your product/service lies on the risk spectrum. If you have multiple products or services, rate each one.

2.   Use that rating to determine the degree to which you need to make the prospect feel you are capable and competent, and the techniques and communication devices you need to employ to attain that determination.

3.   If you are an existing business, analyze your current "first impression" from that point of view, and make whatever changes you need to make to improve it.

4.   If you are just starting, develop your "first impression" based on the ideas described in this chapter.

5.   As is almost always the case, have someone else help you. Because you are very close to these issues, you may not be as objective and detailed as someone else.

5

Making Customers Comfortable in One-on-One Selling Situations

If you have a high-risk offer, that offer puts you into the realm of face-to-face, one-on-one selling. Here, you must develop a positive business relationship with the individual prospect in order to mitigate the risk. That means that your prospect must know you and your company, trust you and your company, and feel comfortable with you and your company.

Note two things: First, every aspect of the relationship is determined by what the customer thinks and feels about you. Remember the last chapter? Your thoughts and feelings about the prospect don't matter. You don't count. The relationship is 100 percent defined by the customer.

Secondly, it is 100 percent your responsibility to create these thoughts, perceptions, and ideas in the mind and heart of the customer.

It is 100 percent your responsibility to create these thoughts, perceptions, and ideas in the mind and heart of the customer.

Seems a bit unfair, doesn't it? On one hand, the relationship is entirely what the customer thinks it is. On the other, it is entirely your responsibility to influence him or her to feel and think about you in certain positive ways. This is not romance, or family, or friends. This is sales, and sales is a proactive endeavor.

That means that what you do—your actions—stimulate reactions from the customer. The customer doesn't buy from you, and then you go and visit them. You must visit them first and act in such a way as to motivate the customer to give you his money for what you have. Your actions stimulate reactions.

This is one of those simple, obvious rules of effective sales that so often becomes lost and forgotten in the daily ebb and flow of a typical busy day.

Sales is a proactive endeavor.

In terms of building a relationship with the customer, that means that if the customer doesn't like you, respect you, and believe you, it's your fault. There are no such things as impossible customers. There are only salespeople who haven't acted in the right ways.

This is one of the key points that distinguishes the great salespeople from the mediocre. Mediocre salespeople think, "I'm going to just be myself."

That would be okay if you were such an engaging, sensitive, and positive personality that everyone—no exception—is immediately comfortable with you and attracted to you. I have yet to find anyone who meets that description. I certainly don't. Even the most universally attractive people rub some people the wrong way.

Unfortunately, if you are going to be good at sales, "being yourself" is not sufficient. For example, if you are an aggressive, loud person who dominates every conversation and speaks over people, you will irritate the vast majority of your customers. And because they won't like you, they will find reasons not to do business with you.

"That's an extreme example," you may be thinking. Perhaps, but it illustrates the point. There are people who will not react well to you being yourself. For some reason, you will just rub some people the wrong way. So, if you insist on "just being yourself," you will eliminate some portion of your market who just won't like you!

Great salespeople know that there is a science to creating positive business relationships. It is far more important to discipline yourself to adhere to the best practices, than it is to "be yourself."

Let's start with that first contact. The question is this: Once you understand that you are in a one-to-one selling situation, how do you make a first impression on your prospect so that he or she feels you are, at least to some degree, capable, credible, and non-threatening?

It begins, of course, with your initial, non-personal contact—all the things that we discussed in the chapter on "interacting" with the right people. If you are sending them a snail mail letter, how does it look? Does the logo and letterhead make you appear capable and credible? Is your punctuation perfect, your grammar understandable, and your spelling error-less?

The same criteria apply to a phone call. Your words, your tone of voice, your cadence, your accent—all combine to create an impression in the prospect.

At some point, though, your prospect will need to see you, eyeball-to-eyeball, in real life. Be early! Five to 10 minutes is appropriate. More than that and you look desperate and present a bit of a problem to the prospect.

Next, pay attention to your appearance. People will form an impression of you, based on how you look before they even say hello to you. Your appearance, then, should be designed to help you look confident and competent—whatever that means in your market. At a minimum, that means clothes clean and pressed, shoes shined, and hair cut.

Your attire should help you connect with the customer—not separate you from him. For example, if you are calling on production supervisors, you should not wear a suit and tie, as that will separate you from them and generate a bit of discomfort in them.

The best rule I've seen is this: Dress like your customer, only a little better. On several occasions, I have worked with sales forces who sold to farmers. Blue jeans and flannel shirts are okay, as long as they are clean and pressed blue jeans, and a better-quality flannel shirt.

But what if you call on several different types of customers in the same day? One salesperson shared his approach to this problem. He wore gray slacks, a blue button-down collared shirt, and a navy blazer. When he called on managers and executives, he dressed it up by putting on a tie. And when he called on people who weren't in the executive suite, he dressed it down by removing the blazer and the tie.

Can you imagine our grant-writing freelancer, upon finally gaining an appointment with a key decision-maker, showing up 10 minutes late and wearing jeans and a sweatshirt?

You can see the point—the grant writer would have lost the prospect before even saying a word. Just as the impact of this poor personal presentation is blatantly obvious to everyone, so too should be the positive impact that paying attention to the details of your first impression will create.

Smile warmly, shake hands firmly, speak slowly, and begin to build rapport immediately. Here are a few ways to build rapport in the initial encounter.

1. **Be polite.** There is a reason why etiquette has been a concern for generations of people. Being polite and sensitive to the other person is more than just good manners—it is good business. Trust me, no one will object to you being polite. Far more will react negatively to your lack of manners.

    ■ Use "Mr." or "Mrs." unless you are older and more established than they are.

    ■ Stand up when shaking hands and upon the customer's entry into the room.

    ■ Say "Please" and "Thank you," ask permission to do anything in their office or facility, and open doors for them.

2. **Try an occasional bit of disarming honesty.**
   In routine interchanges, say something that the
   customer is not expecting. For example, when he
   says, "How are you?" instead of the perfunctory
   "Fine," try something like this: "Honestly, my day
   didn't get off to a good start. One of the kids was
   sick this morning, and I was a half hour late getting out of the house. How are you?"

   It's disarming because it was unexpected. It
   reveals something about you, and describes a situation with which almost everyone can relate. A
   good way to build rapport.

3. **Humor.** If you are one of those people who can
   make most people laugh most of the time, then
   you are equipped with a powerful rapport-building asset. There is something about laughing together that breaks down some of the barriers between people and removes some of the tension.

   If you are not one of those comedy-gifted people then it's better to stay away from this. Telling
   a joke that nobody gets, or having a glib comment
   being seen as sarcastic or caustic is *not* a good
   way to build rapport.

4. **Use a sincere compliment.** Everyone likes to be
   complimented. When you sincerely compliment
   a customer (or his company), you communicate
   that you are interested in him or her, that you
   have noticed something he or she does that stands
   out, and that you aren't afraid to say something
   complimentary. Those are all good things.

Not so long ago, I entered a prospect's office building for the first time. The lobby was a dramatic, two-story atrium with a soaring piece of sculpture. When he came down to meet me, I immediately told him that the lobby was very impressive, and that I felt very comfortable and a bit inspired because of it. We chatted for a few minutes about it and I then followed him to his office, having achieved some rapport.

5. **Ask a perceptive question.** A perceptive question asked with sincerity does everything that a compliment does and then some. When the compliment doesn't call for any response from the customer, a question does. If done correctly, it can initiate the conversation and help the customer feel like you are interested and care about him. In the previous situation, for example, I could have said, "Was it designed to create that kind of feeling?"

6. **Indicate a personal connection.** If you have something in common with the customer, mention it. You don't have to beat it to death, just mention it. When the customer discovers that you both know the same person, went to the same school, vacationed in the same place, or belongs to the same organization, he realizes that you are alike in some ways.

7. **Tell a short personal story.** It doesn't have to be a major digression, but a short story about something personal is a great rapport builder. For example: "Boy, I had a hard time getting

here on time. I must have run over some glass or something sharp, because about half way here, my right front tire went flat. Took me a while to change it. Glad I made it."

That's short, it's personal, and it's a bit transparent, because it reveals something about you as a human being. Plus, it's something to which everyone can relate.

Building rapport is a science with proven practices and tactics. Use any of these techniques and watch your ability to create rapport improve, and thereby smooth out the way to better business relationships.

If your sales situation calls for multiple sales calls and more intense relationships, then you must focus on an additional set of practices that establish trusting, longer-term relationships. The standard now is considerably higher than just conveying a sense of credibility and competence. Your job now is to create a positive business relationship that is characterized by the customer knowing you, your product and your company, trusting you, your product and your company, and feeling comfortable with you.

Here are seven powerful rules to do this better.

1. **Be sincerely interested in them.** In addition, everyone, at some point or another, talks about themselves and their problems. By developing a sincere interest in your customer, you lay the groundwork for a reciprocal response from your customer. You make it easy for them to be comfortable with you.

Discipline yourself to find things to be interested in. Be observant, study their environment, their offices, and their personal presentation to find things that set them off and show them to be unique.

Take notes and keep information about their families, their interests, their political leanings, and so on. Ask questions about their ideas, experiences, and insights. Listen carefully and respond appropriately. That makes it easier for them to be *comfortable* with you.

2. **Share something personal.** People buy from people. People buy from people they know and like. Therefore, if they know and like you, it is easier for them to buy from you. Remember the oil can? Squirt some oil into the process and make it easier for them to do business with you. To do so, be proactive and share something personal about yourself. Force them to recognize you as a unique human being, not just a stereotypical salesperson.

For example, in almost every presentation I make, as I am introducing myself to the audience, I say something like this: "My wife and I had 19 foster children of various sexes and races and physical and emotional disabilities." That statement of something unique and personal about me may seem out of place in a presentation on some aspect of sales to a group of sales professionals. But it serves to set me apart and to send the clear and strong signal that I am a person, a real person, not just a speaker. It is my job to make them comfortable with me, and sharing something personal about myself is one way I do that.

The principle applies to every one-on-one selling situation. That makes them comfortable with you, and implants knowledge of you in their mind.

3. **Bring value to every interaction.** Here's the standard—every time they see you, they must feel as though they have received something of value for the time they spent with you, or they won't want to spend time with you again.

I am astonished at how infrequently this little bit of common sense shows up as part of a professional salesperson's mindset. The overwhelming majority of salespeople concentrate on their agenda, on what they want to accomplish in the sales visit, and never think about what the customer gains from spending time with them.

Remember, sales isn't about you. It's about helping them. See it from their point of view. Why should they invest their valuable time in talking with you?

See it from their point of view. Why should they invest their valuable time in talking with you?

Just asking that question before you plan every sales call will keep the issue at the top of your mind and lead you to a higher level of performance. If you need to think more specifically, here's a list of things that are often seen as valuable by the customer:

- Some good ideas to help him in his business or his job.
- Some ways to help him gain more business.
- Some ways to distinguish himself from others.
- Some ideas about how to reduce his costs.
- Some good things to think about.
- You helped him resolve some conflict.
- You helped him simplify things.
- You helped him solve a problem.
- You helped him move closer to some objective.
- You made him feel better about himself or his business.
- He got to spend face time with you.

4. **Ask good questions and listen constructively.** I'm going to discuss this in much greater detail later in the book. For now, let me make the point that one of the best ways to make people feel good about you is to ask about them. That means you ask thoughtful, sensitive questions about them and their business or their needs, and that you proactively listen and respond.

5. **Do what you say you are going to do.** This is more complex than it may seem. If you are going to be seeing a customer on multiple occasions, you will, as a matter of course, have several opportunities to make a commitment to the customer to do something—send a quote, drop off a sample, e-mail a copy of the recipe you recommended, and

so on. In the heat of the moment, during the sales interaction, it is easy to be accommodating and agree to do all kinds of things.

Be careful about agreeing to do anything that you are not sure you can do. It is better to say no upfront than it is to agree to do something and not follow through.

If you don't do what you say you are going to do, you'll be perceived as not trustworthy—exactly the opposite of what you want.

Give yourself margins in your commitments. For example, if you know you can get a quote back to them on Monday, promise it for Wednesday. That gives you a couple of extra days if something unforeseen comes up. If not, you'll look good by delivering it on Monday, a couple of days ahead of when you promised it.

6. **Be remembered favorably.** Although the relationship with the customer may be at the center of your thoughts, therefore subject to lots of strategizing, preparation, and reflection, the opposite is rarely true. You are rarely given a whole lot of thought by the customer. You are probably not the only salesperson he'll see today, and certainly not the only thing on his agenda. In fact, he may almost totally forget you in a few weeks' time.

Being forgotten, or worse, remembered badly, is a waste of all the time and effort you have put into this relationship so far. It portends badly for the future and your ability to wring any money out of the relationship.

That thought process leads us to a conclusion: We should be remembered, and, if at all possible, remembered favorably.

That's one of the reasons why we try to create rapport with the customer—to create a warm and positive emotional atmosphere. The feelings will often linger beyond the content of the conversation.

If you manage the engagement well by asking good questions, listening constructively, and providing value (all dealt with in later chapters), you'll contribute substantially to that favorable impression.

If you gain agreement with the customer and shake hands at the end of the engagement over an "I'll do this and you'll do that" kind of commitment, you'll go a long way to leaving a favorable impression.

Although we are going to discuss each of these in greater detail later in the book, for now it is sufficient for you to commit (prior to every engagement with the customer) to leaving a favorable impression on the customer. Given that charge, you'll find lots of ways to do so.

7. **Entertain strategically.** If your risk/relationship equation is on the extreme right end of the spectrum, the offer that you make to the customer is huge. Often it is in the nature of "spend millions of dollars with me this year," or "risk your job on my new product," or "let me manage your life

savings," or "let's merge our two companies and go after this market together"—all of which are huge risks.

If that is the world you live in, then you need to add one more tool to your relationship-building tool box. You need to entertain strategically.

Entertaining means creating ways to spend time outside of the business setting with your customers. Entertaining is not giving your customer two tickets to the ball game. It is taking them with you to the ball game.

When you spend social time with your customer, away from the office or the business environment, you come to know one another at different and deeper levels. The relationship expands. Your customer comes to know you more intimately and, as a result, feels more comfortable with you. And that can make all the difference.

In one of my sales positions, I had a huge potential account, but could get nowhere with it. The reason was that the head of purchasing, a middle-aged lady named Linda, did not like me. She thought I was a jerk. For what it is worth, I wasn't particularly fond of Linda, but it didn't matter what I thought. Remember, the relationship is 100 percent defined by the customer. Linda thought I was a jerk, and that was enough to keep the gears of the relationship locked and immobile.

My company had purchased a small local company in Ann Arbor, Michigan. This was a third generation wholesale distributor. With the purchase came all the assets of the company. One of the assets was six season tickets to the University of Michigan football games. At the time, it was the practice of the U of M to allow season ticket holders to get closer every year, as inevitably some ticket holders with better seats did not renew.

For three generations, the owners skootched. Now, the tickets were on the 35 yard line, about 16 rows up. It doesn't get much better than that.

My manager allowed me to use the six tickets for one game. I decided to use them strategically. Looking through my list of high-potential customers, the individual at the top of the list was Linda. So, I invited Linda and her husband to be my guests, with my wife and another couple to the game.

I know that if it weren't for her husband, she would have never agreed. She didn't want to spend an afternoon with me! But she knew that it might be her husband's one and only opportunity in his lifetime to attend a U of M game, on the 35 yard line, 16 rows up.

So we organized the party of six, and we did it to the max. The day began with a tailgate party and continued on through a glorious October afternoon in Ann Arbor with 100,000-plus people attending. It was a wonderful day, because Linda got to know me differently. She made friends with my wife and became much more comfortable with me.

The next week when I called on her, everything was different. The doors opened and throughout the next few years, I did $2 million–plus in sales for that account.

The moral of the story? When the risk is big, the relationship needs to be correspondingly significant. If you are in a high-risk selling situation, entertain your customers.

We have assembled a variety of resources to help you accomplish this step of the process. Visit *http://www.sellanythingtoanyone. net/comfortable.php* to review them.

How to Implement the Ideas in This Chapter

1. It is 100 percent your responsibility to create thoughts, perceptions, and ideas in the mind and heart of the customer.
2. Sales is a proactive endeavor.
3. Decide how to dress in a first visit.
4. Pick a couple of the eight rapport-building tactics that seem to fit you and practice them.
5. Study the seven relationship-building strategies and discipline yourself to implement them.
6. Ask yourself, before every face-to-face visit: "Why should they invest their valuable time in talking with me?"

6

Finding Out
What Customers Want

Selling is not manipulating people so that they take something they don't want. Instead, it is finding out what they already want and appealing to that interest. The best salespeople excel at this step in the process.

I believe this step is at the heart of selling—the essence of what sales is all about. I know that flies in the face of the routine practices who believe that the end-all of their focus is to push their product.

You can proclaim the merits of your product to willing and unwilling listeners and Webpage visitors far and wide, attempting to sway them with the powerful features and advantages that your product offers over the competition. Unfortunately, it is that approach that has given a bad name to salespeople.

On the other hand, you can focus on the customer, finding out what motivates her, what issues are important to her, what problems she has, what objectives she is trying to solve, and what she looks for in a vendor, and then appeal to that motivation.

Everything that you have done prior to this is designed to get to this understanding. And everything that you do afterward is based on this step. It is the fulcrum upon which the entire sales process pivots.

Finding out what they want is the fulcrum upon which the entire sales process pivots.

Let's look at some of our basic scenarios to gain an understanding of this step, beginning with the coffee shop. As the coffee shop owner, you've methodically worked through the first two steps and have now decided that your potential customers want hot, cheap coffee quickly. So, you set up a system whereby you pre-pour 10 cups at a time and hand them to people in their cars in return for a one-dollar bill. (Out-of-the box-thinking.) You congratulate yourself on your creativity.

But, alas, it didn't go over well. It turns out that your market (the right people) doesn't so much want cheap, quick coffee as they want the ability to customize it, and will pay two or three times more for that ability.

Now you have a real problem. Because you were sure your out-of-the-box idea would be big, you didn't get a space large enough to serve more than one customer at a time. It takes you a while to serve each person, which means lines quickly form. Because most of your people don't like to stand in line for long, your business is suffering. What's the problem? When you thought you knew what they wanted, you didn't get it right. That puts everything in jeopardy.

This little scenario uncovers one of the pitfalls that eventually ruins many entrepreneurs. It occurs when they happen on an idea that enamors them. They love it, and because they love it, they think everyone else will, too. They become passionate and committed, quit the day job, mortgage the family home, and invest huge amounts of time and energy into the new idea.

Time after time, I've seen this passionate enthusiasm turn to frustration as the new idea limps along, draining the entrepreneurs' passion, energy, and money. It turns out that not enough people wanted it as much as the entrepreneur thought they would want it. He judged the market by his enthusiasm, and his enthusiasm was inexperienced and misplaced.

For example, a client of mine had developed an idea: a small electronic device that would be placed in the homes of parents of children who rode the bus to school. It would emit a loud alert when the school bus was a block or so away and approaching their stop. What a great idea! Kids wouldn't have to wait out for the bus in inclement weather when the bus was late, and parents wouldn't worry. He spent years perfecting the technology, creating the marketing collateral, and attempting to sell it. I was called in when the money was almost gone and the product still had not sold.

The problem was the classic problem I described previously. Although some of the parents thought it was a good idea, it wasn't good enough for them to pay for it. The bus drivers hated it because it was just one more thing for them to do. The transportation supervisors saw it as an expensive technology that they would have to maintain. And the school boards never found slack in their budgets to allow them to purchase it. Years of effort, hundreds of thousands of dollars, bucket loads of passion and emotional energy—all down the tube. Why? Because the prospects didn't want it.

Or at least they didn't want it enough to pay the price and take the risk. Now we have uncovered another significant principle. They may say they want it, but they need to want it enough to pay the price and assume the risk.

They may say they want it, but they need to want it enough to pay the price and assume the risk.

The parents thought it was a good idea. But what happens if they forget to recharge it and it doesn't go off. Or if the kids are watching the TV and they don't hear it go off? Or the driver forgets to push the button? Then, of course, the parents have a bigger problem—how to get the kids to school when they've missed the bus. They would just rather not take that risk.

The drivers saw it as all risk and no reward. What happens to them if they forget to push the button? Irate parents calling all day.

The transportation supervisors thought it was a good idea until they considered what they would have to deal with if the thing didn't work or the drivers forgot to push the button. They decided the risk of all those calls from angry parents wasn't worth it.

In this case no one saw the benefit as being worth the risk. In other words, it didn't adequately fill any need or want. The entrepreneur wasted years of effort on this one, because he never verified the strength of the want of the people to whom it was appealing.

The real problem occurs when we project our thoughts and feelings onto the customer and assume that he or she wants something just because we do. There is a difference between assumed wants and verified wants. When we assume that the customer wants something, particularly if we have little evidence to validate that assumption, we are on very shaky ground. We may be right, but the odds are against us. It's the coffee shop entrepreneur who assumed that his customers wanted fast, cheap coffee, because that would appeal to him. Alas, they weren't him.

It is far better to verify what they really do want. Once again, it really isn't an either/or situation, but rather gradations of one or the other. Here's our spectrum again, this time reflecting the validity you can attribute to various ways of ascertaining what they want.

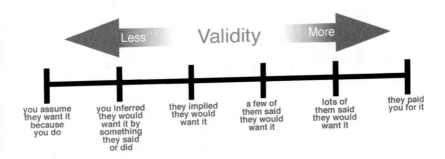

The further we go to the right in our source of information, the more we can bank on the validity of the information. For example, our coffee shop entrepreneur started out on the far left, assuming that because the idea of hot, cheap coffee appealed to him, it would appeal to everyone else. Although he didn't get an idea of what they wanted, he got a clear picture of what they didn't want!

You can see how incredibly important it is to accurately and verifiably "find out what they want." So, how do you do this?

Let's use the spectrum to guide us. You can infer that they want something, because you know they want something else. For example, if you have a Website selling gourmet tea imported from seven locations around the world, you infer that the people who want that tea would also want tea cups. Because they are willing to pay more for their tea, you infer that they would also be willing to pay more for their tea cups, so you consider bringing in a line of expensive, artisan tea cups.

Next, you can ask them in several ways: You can send them a survey, either on paper or electronically. If you ask the right question and enough of them respond positively, you are on safer ground than if you just inferred it. You could, for example, send a quick two-question survey to everyone who ordered your tea on the Web and ask them if they buy tea cups and would they pay this much for one.

Another way to ask them is through the mechanism of a focus group. You bring a group of them together, expose them to what you have, and have them share their feelings and thoughts with each other and you. This is best done by a professional. So, if you are anticipating this, set some money aside and have it done by someone who knows what they are doing.

You can also use an informal survey. Call a bunch of your friends and ask them. Better yet, run the idea by some people who you don't know so well.

Although all these ideas have merit, they are primarily reliable when done in big numbers by professional firms who know exactly how to do it. Done informally, they have their limitations. People will tell you things, sometimes with great certainty, which are just not true.

When I wrote my first book, it was self-published to a niche market. We sent a short summary of the book to several hundred of the potential customers and asked them if they would buy it for their salespeople. Then we asked them how many they would buy.

When we started to market the book, the first people we appealed to were those folks who said "Yes. This is the greatest idea since sliced bread. I'd buy one for every salesperson." Of those who fervently and intensely said yes in the survey, about 1 in 20 actually wrote a check. There is a huge gap between what people say they would do, and what they actually will do. In the world of sales, talk truly is cheap.

Although it may be a little more emotionally painful, if you are selling to potentially lots of people, as in a Website or retail store, you may find it cost effective to put a small amount of "it" out there, and see if the customers want it enough to pay for it. So, instead of asking them if they would buy these expensive tea cups for X dollars, actually put an ad for them on your Website and see if people really do buy them. Pay very close attention, measure the results daily, and don't be afraid to act when you get an idea of which way the trend is going.

Our coffee shop entrepreneur, for example, made an initial mistake by assuming what his customers would want, he quickly read the market and attempted to switch gears. The behavior of the customers—and what they showed they would and would not pay for—probably brought him better information and at a lower cost than if he had done a focus group or surveyed 300 prospects.

With just a little bit of thought, you'll arrive at a question that uncovers another complication. What's the likelihood of all of your customers wanting the same thing?

If you are selling something really basic, such as groceries, chances are pretty good. But as you start to move away from the most basic commodities, let's say to "imported gourmet groceries," you'll begin to part with vast groups of your prospects. That idea brings us to this: Your market is always made up of a mix of segments or niches. To find out what your customers want, break them up into smaller segments and find out what each segment wants.

> **To find out what your customers want, break them up into smaller segments and find out what each segment wants.**

Let's use our coffee shop as an example. You, the owner, are having some problems. Your hot, cheap coffee idea didn't go as planned and you are having trouble serving people in the store. "What do they want?" you wonder in frustration. A flash of enlightenment comes out of the blue as you have this thought: "Why not ask them?"

So, you put together a little form with a question on it:

"At this time of day, what would be your ideal coffee experience?"

You decide that you are going to ask every customer that comes by and note the answers.

At the end of the day as you consider the responses, you realize that different types of people wanted different things. Early in the morning, from 7 a.m. to 8:30 a.m., most of your customers were office workers on their way to their jobs at the office park down the street. They wanted coffee quickly, but they also wanted something a little special about it (they could get a basic cup of coffee at the office), and they wanted it served with a warm smile. That is your first segment.

Later in the day, your customers were mostly housewives and business people looking for a pleasant place to pass some time. That's your second segment.

You also notice a significant contingent of students who would come in with friends and occupy a couple of tables for an hour or so. They wanted space and no pressure to move on. Another segment.

Notice that if you put all their wants into one big basket, it would be very confusing. However, when you broke your market up into segments, the picture became clearer.

No matter what you are selling, if your sales situation is populated with lots of customers, you will always understand them better if you break them down into component segments.

As you search for ways to classify your prospects and customers, be driven by this question: What are the most important ways they have things in common? "Important" means important to your business and to your sales situation. What might be important to you in your coffee shop, for example, may have absolutely no relevance to the tea-selling Website.

Think, first, about what they do. In our coffee shop example, we have office workers, business people, and students. One of my clients wanted to expand his business with farmers. There was a natural separation into crop growers, fruit growers, dairy farms, and other livestock farms.

Think also about demographics. Things such as age, sex, educational background, location, and so on. Usually a combination of these is most illuminating. For example, there might be little to be gained by breaking our coffee shop customers up into male and female. It would be far more instructive if we said males from 20 to 35 years of age, females from 35 to 50.

Once you think you know what a segment wants, write it down in no more than 75 words. The process of writing it down will force you to clarify it, and the 75 words will ensure that you are focusing on the essentials and not wandering off in tangents.

Now, if you have broken your market up into several smaller component segments and you have a clear, written statement of what each segment wants, and you have some verification that they really do want that, then you have done this well. You're ready to move on.

Remember where we started out at the beginning of this chapter? This step is the fulcrum upon which the whole sales process pivots. It is so important that, if you can't say with clarity and precision what your market wants, you should not move forward. Any success you might have without this will be pure luck.

Note: We have assembled a variety of resources to help you accomplish this step of the process. Visit *http://www. sellanythingtoanyone.net/findout.php* to review them.

How to Implement the Ideas in This Chapter

1. Review the spectrum on page 102, and use it to guide your decision.
2. Create a system that captures, as accurately as possible, "what they want."

3. Create the tools necessary to make the system work.

4. Put that system in place and begin to capture, as objectively as possible, measurable expressions of what your customers want.

5. Review that system regularly to make sure that you are capturing accurate information.

7

What Customers Want in One-on-One Selling Situations

In the previous chapter, I asserted that this step is the most important step. It is the fulcrum upon which the entire sales process pivots. That is just as true in one-on-one sales situations as it is in the mass market selling situations of the previous chapter. The difference, though, is dramatic. Whereas in mass market situations you want to find out what a lot of people want, generally in sort of a superficial way in one-on-one selling you want to find out what this particular person wants, and not only for himself, but often for the organization that he represents as well.

When it comes to one-on-one selling, I have come to the conclusion that this skill—the skill of finding out what the customer wants—is the highest and best of all the sales competencies. Great salespeople excel at this and mediocre salespeople are dismal at it.

As the buyer, when you find yourself interacting with a salesperson who doesn't ask questions, understand that you are in the hands of a mediocre salesperson. Your chances of having a satisfactory experience are no better than pure luck.

A number of years ago, a major non-profit professional association did a study of the behavioral characteristics of the best salespeople, regardless of what they sold. Among those behaviors that the best shared was this: They ask better questions and listen more constructively.

Imagine that. Something as simple as asking better questions and listening better separated the very best from the also-rans. Although that may be an amazing idea to a lot of people, it is not to you and me. That's because we understand that sales is a process, and in order to do sales well, you need to execute every step of the process, and execute each as thoroughly and effectively as possible.

Naturally, then, those people who do each step and do so well are much more effective than those who try to skip a step.

That brings us to an important observation. In one-on-one sales situations, a good question is your most powerful sales tool.

> **In one-on-one sales situations, a good question is your most powerful sales tool.**

Let's examine some of the reasons why a good question is your most powerful tool.

1. **A good question directs the customer's thinking.** "Did you enjoy what you had for breakfast this morning?"

   Now consider what you did when you read that question. In a split second, you conjured up a picture of you eating breakfast this morning. You reviewed that by considering the picture, and then made a judgment about it: You either did or did not enjoy it.

   In other words, my question caused you to think a certain way about a certain subject. And every person who reads this book will do exactly the same thing. My question will direct and influence the thinking process of thousands of people in some small way.

   Every good question that you ask in a sales encounter will, in some way, direct the customer's thinking. The way you get him to think about something is to ask him about it. When you ask a question, your customer thinks of the answer. In some small way, that makes you in charge of his thinking processes.

   If you are our grant-writing freelancer, for example, you could ask a prospect a question like this: "How important are outside funds to the health and viability of your organization?"

   That would get him thinking about the subject that you wanted to discuss with him.

2. **A good question collects a certain quantity and quality of information.** How else can you find out what the customer really wants unless you ask him? Your ability to understand what the customer wants is a direct result of your ability to ask him questions that uncover that understanding.

Our freelancer could follow the previous question with one designed to uncover some important information like this: "If you look at the income of which you are sure and compare it to your budget, what is the short fall? How much do you have to raise through other outside sources?"

3. **A good question enhances relationships.** When someone asks you about yourself and your company, your challenges and your aspirations, you naturally respond positively to that person's interest in you. You feel good about the other person, because that question demonstrated an interest in you. We all like people to be interested in us.

Therefore, when you ask good questions and show sincere interest in the other person, it influences him to feel good about you.

4. **A series of good questions create the perception of your competence.** At some intuitive level, we all understand that it takes more competence with a subject to be able to ask about it than it does to be able to talk about it.

Here's an example. Suppose you're having difficulty with your automobile, so you take it in to the mechanic down the street. You notice a neon sign in his window announcing "computer diagnostics." On the walls of his reception room hang several certificates.

"I'm having trouble with my car," you say. "It's making a funny noise."

"We're all certified," he says, "and we have computer diagnostics. Leave it here and pick it up at 5 p.m."

You aren't totally sold, so you go across the street to the competing mechanic there. You notice there is no sign in the window, nor certificates on the wall.

You say the same thing to the mechanic. "I'm having trouble with my car. It's making a funny noise."

"What kind of noise?" he asks.

"It's a strange thumping sound," you reply.

"Can you describe it?"

"It sounds like something metal banging against something else."

"Where is it coming from?"

"Someplace in the front. It sounds like more to the passenger side of the car."

"What kind of car do you have?" he asks.

"2008 Taurus."

"'2008 Taurus, huh. Okay, tell me, when you drive faster, does the thumping increase its rate also?"

"Well, now that you mention it, I believe it does."

"Okay," he says. "And do you hear the sound when the car is cold, just after you start it in the morning, as well as when it's hot?"

"Actually," you say, "I don't think it does happen when it's cold."

"Okay," he says, "Leave it here and pick it up at 5 p.m."

Which one of the two mechanics do you leave your car with? Silly question. Everyone I know says they'd leave it with the second mechanic. Why? Because he obviously knows what he's doing.

And what made you think that he knows what he's doing?

It's his questions! He demonstrated his competence by the questions he asked. We understand that it takes greater competence to ask good questions about a situation than it does to make pithy statements.

5. **A good question helps the customer understand his or her values.** When you ask a question such as, "Which of these three things is most important to you?" you are asking the customer to

clarify his values. He may never have done that before.

I was shopping for a car with my wife. Eventually, we encountered a good car salesperson. We recognized that he was good because he took the time to ask us what we were looking for before he began to pitch a car to us. When he found out we were looking for a car for my wife, he addressed his questions to her. One question, a good sales question, was this:

"Mrs. Kahle, which would you rather have? A car that is quick and sporty and fun to drive, or one that is more comfortable and more stable?" She thought for a moment and then answered, "I have had sporty, so I'm ready for comfortable."

She did not know that until she was asked a good question by a good salesperson that forced her to process life experiences and values and feelings, and when she rolled them all together and voiced a position, she knew what she wanted. The salesperson did us a service by asking a question that helped her sort out her values.

See how powerful a good sales question can be? That's why it is the single-most powerful sales tool you will have.

But we are not just interested in using good questions. We want to create better questions. For a full explanation of what constitutes a better sales question, I'd recommend you read my book, *Question Your Way to Sales Success* (Career Press).

In the meantime, here's one powerful principle that separates an ordinary question from a better sales question: A better sales question digs deeper.

A better sales question digs deeper.

Let me illustrate. You and your spouse decide to make a big salad for dinner. He or she suggests that you prepare the onion.

So, you get out a big, fat Bermuda onion. You position it carefully on a cutting board and root through the drawer until you find a sharp meat cleaver. Steadying the onion with one hand, you raise the meat cleaver above your head and with a karate-type movement, smash the meat cleaver neatly into the center of the onion, splitting it evenly in two.

You pick up one of the onion halves and examine it from the inside. You note that it has layers and layers, each deeper and more tightly compressed than the one surrounding it. You begin to peel the onion, stripping off the skin. As you pull off the skin of the onion, you notice that the skin is thin, dry, and crinkly, with very little scent.

However, as you peel each layer one at a time, you soon come to the conclusion that each layer is more strongly scented than the layer above it, and that the strength of the onion's pungency comes from the inside out. Got the image?

Good. That's the best way to understand this principle. Just like there are layers and layers to an onion, so there are layers and layers to your customer. Just like the superficial layers of an onion are thin and mild, the superficial levels of your customer's have little strength. But as you peel the onion deeper and deeper, the strength increases. This is true about your customers as well.

Look at the following illustration. It represents a simplified onion with its layers and levels. At the most superficial level, like the skin of the onion, is the customer's most superficial problems *or objectives.*

The second layer down consists of the *implications.* In other words, you take the time to understand the consequences of successfully solving the problem or meeting the objective, as well as the consequences of not doing so. You probe those consequences or implications on the company, as well as the individuals with whom you are working.

For example, you may have discovered that a customer wants to increase the production capacity by 5 percent. When you enter into a discussion with her that causes you to understand the consequences of not increasing capacity, and the ramifications of doing so, that's good. When you understand what those consequences are for the individuals within the company, you've just peeled the onion a little deeper.

For example, your customer may say, "If we don't get the 5-percent increase in capacity, we'll not be able to handle the new contract from Ford. And if we can't handle the new contract, they could very well take our current business away from us, because they want to consolidate vendors. That's a major portion of our business. If that goes, we'd have a difficult time surviving." Now that you know the consequences on the company, you've discovered the *implication* level of the onion.

Peeling further may result in your customer sharing the implications for him: "I may not have a job."

Now, let's peel the onion one more level, and discover the emotional level. How do the implications make the individuals within that company feel? When your customer confides in you that he or she would feel "really proud" to have helped achieve that increase, and "scared about what might happen" if the increase is not achieved, you will have peeled the onion in a very significant, powerful way. You now understand the customer probably better than any of your competitors, because you've focused on understanding the customer's PIE.

The world is full of mediocre salespeople who are content to ask superficial questions and get superficial responses. The better salespeople dig deeper with deeper questions, and come to understand what the customer wants at deeper levels.

As always, though, the question is: "How do you implement these principles?" The answer?

Preparing Good Sales Questions

When you're making a presentation, you don't always have to perfectly phrase everything you say. People will understand what you mean even if you're not totally accurate in your choice of words. It's acceptable to say, "About 50 percent" instead of saying "49.27 percent."

That, however, is not the case when you're phrasing questions. The language in your question must be perfect, because the words in your question direct your prospect's thinking. A little change in words can make a huge difference in your prospect's response.

I had created a telemarketing program for one of my clients and stopped in to follow up with him a couple of months after the program was instituted.

"How's it going?" I asked.

"Fine," he said, "the telemarketers are creating lots of leads." "But," he said, "I have a problem."

"What's your problem?" I asked.

"I can't get the salespeople to follow up on the leads," he replied. "So I have a question."

"What's the question?" I asked.

"How can I get the salespeople to follow up on the leads?"

I thought for a moment and replied, "I think that's the wrong question."

"What should I ask?" he said.

"How can I get the leads followed up on?" I responded.

Let's consider what happened. When he asked, "How can I get the salespeople to follow up on the leads," our thinking was directed to the salespeople. The solution to his problem would be limited to salespeople.

However, when we changed the question to, "How can I get the leads followed up on?" we opened up a much larger range of possibilities. Maybe the telemarketers could follow up on them, maybe the owner or sales manager could, maybe the salespeople could, and maybe some independent reps could. We opened the door to a world of possible solutions.

You see, the tiny change in wording in the phrasing of the question caused an enormous change in the direction of our thinking, and, therefore, a major shift in the solutions that followed.

That's why it's important to phrase your key questions word-for-word to make certain that they are exactly what you want them to be.

You'll be much more likely to phrase your questions accurately if you spend time preparing them first than if you attempt to do all your composing on the spur of the moment. That's not to say that you'll never create impromptu questions during the interaction with your customer. Of course you will. But you need to have your basic questions prepared before your meeting starts.

By taking the time to prepare questions first, you can be certain that they are the most effective you can make them.

Step 1: Frame the situation

Begin by thinking about the situation you'll be encountering. Take a few moments and construct it in your mind. For example, you may be meeting a new prospect for the first time. Imagine the setting, see the situation, and envision the person.

Then think about what you want to accomplish in that situation. Let's use our freelance grant writer as an example. That's you, and you have managed to acquire an appointment with a key person in one of your target organizations. Although it would be great if you were to walk out of the meeting with a project, that is probably not going to happen. So, what do you want to achieve in this first meeting? You might have identified these objectives:

- To uncover the prospect's needs and interests as it relates to acquiring additional funds for the organization.
- To qualify him as a potential buyer.
- To begin to develop a trusting relationship with him.
- To share enough information with him that he will be willing to see me again at a later date.

Now that you have both the situation and your objectives in mind, it's time to begin to develop questions that will take you where you want to go.

Step 2: Brainstorm all the possibilities

Write down all the questions that you think you might ask. Don't worry about editing them at this point, just get as many questions down on paper as they come into your mind. As you create your questions, keep the two basic types in mind: open-ended and close-ended. An open-ended question is one which can't be answered by just one word. It calls for an explanation, and there is no right or wrong answer. A close-ended question is just the opposite—it calls for a specific bit of information. So, for example, "How do you feel about our proposal?" is an open-ended question, while "Who got the order?" is a close-ended question. Each has a place in the hands of an effective salesperson.

If you are the freelance grant writer, you may come up with these:

1. "Why did you take the time to see me now?"
2. "How important are outside funds to the health and viability of your organization?"
3. "If you look at the guaranteed income, and compare it to your budget, what is the short fall? How much do you have to raise through other outside sources?"
4. "How successful have you been in the past when acquiring grants?"
5. "How have you done it in the past?"
6. "What would be the process you would need to use to hire someone like myself?"
7. "What is the next step?"

Step 3: Edit and refine

After you have created an exhaustive list, go back over it and rewrite those questions that make the most sense to you. Judge each question by these three rules.

1. **A good sales question doesn't intimidate the customer, imply blame, or cause him/her to lose face.** In the past you may have written this question: "What do you dislike about your current supplier?" Bad question. If the person you're speaking to is the same one who selected that supplier, then you're asking him to admit a mistake he has made. That question implies blame and causes the customer, if he were to answer it honestly, to lose face. Rephrase the question to something similar to this: "What qualities or behaviors would you really like to see in a supplier?" That question will bring you the same information as the first one, but will do so in a positive, non-threatening way.

2. **A good sales question prompts the kind of thinking you want.** Let's say you just presented your proposal. One of the questions you've thought about asking is, "Was there anything in the proposal we didn't address?" That question directs the customer to think about what is wrong with the proposal. Suppose you were to rephrase the question to: "How do you think this proposal will benefit you?" In that case, you've directed the customer to think about the positive aspects of the proposal. When you edit your list

of questions, make sure they prompt the kind of thinking you want.

3. **A good sales question asks for the level of information appropriate to the depth of the relationship.** As you deepen your relationship with a customer, you can ask deeper questions. Those questions may be totally inappropriate at the onset of a relationship, but perfectly appropriate when you've established some trust and comfort with your customer.

For example, you may want to ask your customer, "How well entrenched is the competition in your organization?" But that question won't prompt an honest answer until you've created a deeper relationship with the customer.

That's why great salespeople are so good at building relationships. Their relationships allow them to know their customers deeper, and that deeper knowledge enables them to present attractive solutions.

Back to our grant writer. You reflect on the set of questions you created previously and make some "editing" decisions. You think that your first question is just a bit too aggressive for someone you are meeting for the first time, so you decide to eliminate it.

Then you decide to soften questions 4 and 5 a bit by combining them into this: "To what degree have you been successful in acquiring outside funding in the past?"

You like the rest of them and you like the sequence, so you rewrite these:

1. "How important are outside funds to the health and viability of your organization?"

2. "If you look at the income of which you are sure and compare it to your budget, what is the short fall? How much do you have to raise through other outside sources?"

3. "To what degree have you been successful in acquiring outside funding in the past?"

4. "What would be the process you would need to use to hire someone like myself?"

5. "What is the next step?"

Step 4: Develop an effective sequence

Now that you've edited your questions to the point where each question is as good as you can make it, sort them into the sequence you think will be most effective.

The sequence you use can be almost as important as the language of your questions. For example, you'll almost always want to start at the surface of the onion, asking questions about the most general and superficial subjects, and then gradually work your way into the heart of the onion with more pointed questions.

After you go through this process of creating good sales questions a few times, you'll find that you're using some questions over and over. Those good, comfortable questions can be in your tool box as "stock" questions that you can use repetitively.

Some questions that I've found to be particularly effective include: "What can you tell me about your business?" "What's your situation?" "What would have to change for us to do more business with you?"

Step 5: Practice

Just one more little effort will add the icing to the cake and take you a long way to becoming a master. Practice the questions once or twice. It'll only take a minute or two of your time. You'll be sure that the phrasing is comfortable for you, and the practice will help plant the questions in your mind.

With that, you're ready to use the single-most powerful interpersonal tool in your tool box—a good sales question.

Note: We have assembled a variety of resources to help you accomplish this step of the process. Visit *http://www. sellanythingtoanyone.net/findout.php* to review them.

How to Implement the Ideas in This Chapter

Create some better sales questions for your important one-on-one sales calls by following this process:

1. Envision the situation.
2. Brainstorm some questions, word-for-word.
3. Edit and refine them.
4. Develop an effective sequence.
5. Practice them.

8

Show Customers How What You Have Gives Them What They Want

Now at last, we get to what most people think of when they think of "selling": Pitching your product. The idea brings up images of TV infomercials or the guy at the flea market demonstrating the latest thing.

Although those are visible examples of this step in the process, they represent only a tiny slice of all the possible expressions of this practice. This is the step of the process where you talk about what you have to offer and why the customer should invest his or her money buying it from you.

We see examples every day—from a product's label design on the hardware store shelf, to the description of a meal on a restaurant menu, to the display of products in a grocery store, to the description of a product for sale on a Website, to the grant-writing freelancer explaining why he should be hired to do a project. In every one of these examples, and countless millions of others, the sellers are trying to show the customer that what he has gives the customer what he wants—at a price that is worth the risk.

If you have done a good job of engaging with the right people, making them comfortable with you, and finding out what they want, then showing them how what you have gives them what they want is as simple and natural as a knife through warm butter. If what you have doesn't help them get what they want, you either have the wrong thing, or you are talking to the wrong person.

This brings us to the fundamental principle of "showing them how what you have gives them what they want." "Matching" means that the more precisely your offer matches what the customer wants, the more likely you are to make a sale.

> **The more precisely your offer matches what they want, the more likely you are to make a sale.**

Again, this is one of the places where mediocre salespeople have made a bad name for the profession. They proclaim the features of their products to whoever will listen, and hope that, like mud thrown against the wall, some will stick.

I had a personal experience with this exact topic. We had a major remodeling project in mind and invited several contractors to quote the project. One came and seemed very professional. We walked the two representatives of the company through the house, indicating what we wanted done—some work on the bathroom, maybe a redo of one of the bedrooms, and a sliding glass door with a deck off the second-floor living room. As we finished, I told the contractor that we had a budget of $45,000 and asked if he thought he could do it within that range. He said yes, no problem. On the basis of that we gave him a couple of hundred dollars to do a detailed proposal and graphic illustration of how it would look.

When we arrived a few days later to review the finished work, the salesperson presented us with a plan for $60,000 that did not include the sliding glass doors and the deck. I was so angry. They had wasted my time and my money and didn't come close to presenting to me what I had clearly wanted. My conclusion: Either this company was totally incompetent, or deeply deceitful. In either case, I was not going to do business with them. If they had just matched their presentation to my clearly expressed needs, they would have gotten the business.

Let's go back to our coffee shop. Once you understand that a segment of your customers wants hot, quick coffee that is better or different than what they can get at the office, you can create a sign that offers them: Great Flavor! (four different flavors of organic, Costa Rican coffee) Low Price! ($1.50 for an 8-ounce cup), and Quick Service! (30 seconds at a drive through window.) Perfect! Bingo! You are making sales. You presented them with exactly what they wanted at a price and time that was worth the risk. You matched their needs with your offer.

Let's use our tea-selling Website for another example. Here, you have determined that a small segment of your market would probably be interested in a distinctive way to serve their tea, that is, your deal on expensive tea cups. So you bring in a line of imported hand-crafted tea cups, post detailed pictures of them on the Website, and offer them in sets of four. Your promotional text emphasizes the hand-crafted aspects of the product, and you even have a couple of pictures of craftsmen making the tea cups.

Oops, a tactical error! Although you were enamored with the hand-crafted aspect of the tea cups, your customers weren't so much interested in that as they were in the cups themselves. To your customers, it was less about the process of manufacturing than it was about the quality of the product. They saw the craftsmen in simple conditions in a developing country as an indication of the crudity of the product and decided not to buy. Notice that it wasn't the product that was the problem; it was the way it was presented. The presentation wasn't a good match.

In order to do a good job of matching our offer to the customers' needs, we need to understand two fundamental pieces of the equation: Features and Benefits.

Features is the name for the describable characteristics of your offer. *Benefits* is the impact those features have on the customer.

> **Features is the name for the describable characteristics of your offer. Benefits is what call the impact those features have on the customer.**

Features answer questions such as these:

■ What is it?
■ What does it do?
■ What is it made of?
■ How is it different?

Benefits answer questions such as these:

■ So what?
■ What's in it for me?

Let's go back to our coffee shop sign. You decided to put a sign on the curb from 6:30 a.m. to 9:30 a.m. every week day. The sign says "Great Flavor! Low Price! Quick Service!"

"Great Flavor" is a benefit. It is what your features—four different flavors of organic, Costa Rican coffee—mean to the customer. Notice that "four different flavors" "organic," and "Costa Rican" are all describable characteristics of the product. You could verify each one of those statements if you needed. However, "Great Flavor" is what those combinations of features means to the customer. That is much more subjective. In fact, some of your customers may not agree with that statement. But you are betting that most of them will agree with it.

To continue, you can say that the price of $1.50 is a feature, as is the size; an "8-ounce cup." Combined, you hope that the customer will interpret that as "Low Price!" "Low price" is the benefit—what it means to the customer, while $1.50 for an 8-ounce cup is the feature.

Notice that the benefit rises out of the features and interprets them for the most likely impact on the customers.

> **The benefit rises out of the features and interprets them for the most likely impact on the customers.**

One of the fundamental truths of sales is this: People buy benefits, not features. They don't buy your new invention because it is neat; they buy it for what it will do for them.

> **People buy benefits, not features.**

It shows that your presentation, when you tell them how that what you have gives them what they want, should be primarily focused on what they want—the benefits your offer will bring to them. The features are useful to support and provide credence for the benefits, but the benefits are what motivate people to take action.

Let's do some work with this. The following is a list of some common products with features and benefits clearly described.

Product	Feature	Benefit
Ballpoint pen	New type of floating ball in the tip	Easier for you to write
Universal remote	Accommodates five different TVs	You can use one instead of five; saves you money and hassle
Frozen pizza	Heats in a microwave	You can prepare it quickly
New automobile	Built-in GPS	You'll never get lost again

Notice that each of the benefit statements includes the word *you*. That's not necessary, but it does act as a discipline to make sure that you are describing a benefit and not a feature. Remember, benefits are always about the customer, while features are about your product.

Here's another tip to help ensure that your presentation includes a predominance of benefits over features: Mention a feature and then follow it with the phrase (either stated or implied) "this means that you...." What follows is almost always a benefit. So, "Our new automobile has a built in GPS (this means that you) will never get lost again."

Your presentation should emphasize benefits and use features to back up and support the benefits.

One more pertinent observation: You generally have far more features than you can possibly present. In my seminars, I'll sometimes do this exercise: I'll have everyone write down 10 features of their product or service. Then, when they are finished, I'll have them double the number of features. And when they have done that, I'll have them double the number again. Very few have difficulty doing it. When you begin to think about all the things you can possibly say about your product—it's origin, how it's packaged, who makes it, how it's made, what it's made of, who sells it, and so on—you soon have an overwhelming list.

Your customers are not interested in all that. All they want to know is how your product or service helps them get what they want. That means that you need to prioritize and select a handful of features that most closely approximates what the customer wants.

Here, then, is how you can best create the content of your message:

1. Start with a clear description of what your customers want.
2. Carefully consider all the features of your product/service and select those that most directly impact those needs.
3. Turn those features into benefit statements.
4. Begin your presentation with the benefits and use the features to support and add credence to your benefits.

5. Repeat this process with each segment and product/ service you want to sell.

Let's use our coffee shop as an example. You have decided that the early-morning commuter segment wants coffee that is better and different than they can get at the office; they don't want to pay a lot for it; and they don't want to spend a lot of time in the transaction.

As you think about your coffee, you created this partial list of features:

- Freshly made.
- Purified water.
- Organically grown.
- Free-traded.
- From Costa Rica.
- Four different flavors of beans.
- Freshly ground every day.
- Beans are never more than a year old from date of picking.
- Roasted locally.
- Grown in coffee plantations high in the mountains.
- Acquired from a distributor who specializes in Latin American coffee.
- Every lot personally inspected by you our owners.

Whew! All that for a cup of coffee! That is way too much to try to communicate to the customer. So, you prioritize those features that most immediately and directly impact what the customer wants—something different and something better.

You come to this list:

- Four different flavors
- Organically grown
- Costa Rican coffee

Then you turn that into a benefit—"Great Flavor!" and list the salient features beneath that first statement:

> **Great Flavor!**
>
> **Four different flavors of organically grown, Costa Rican coffee.**

See how easy this is? But wait. Now that you have the message, you need to determine the best way to communicate that message. Should you print it on a banner and tie it to the front of your store? Should you advertise it in the local shopping paper? Should you create a Website? Should you put signs up inside the store? Should you create a flier and have a teenager distribute them to the office building? The choices of the medium to communicate your message are overwhelming.

> **The medium should be one with which your customers are currently comfortable.**

Let's discuss some principles: First, the medium should be one with which your customers are currently comfortable.

In other words, you may be entranced by the possibility of creating a neat iPhone application that will drive people to your store but, chances are, not enough of your potential customers would use it to warrant the cost. It doesn't have to be the latest technology! Its better to make it a technology or methodology with which they are currently comfortable.

For example, in my business, my sweet spot in terms of customer segments is a 45- to 65-year-old CEO or vice president of sales. Believe it or not, those folks don't spend a lot of time surfing the Web. Relying strictly on electronic marketing to that demographic would be a disaster. So we use a combination of marketing mediums, including direct mail, telephone calls, articles in hard-copy publications, as well as electronic media.

Another principle: The medium should match the message. The more complex the message, the more intense the media.

The medium should match the message. The more complex the message, the more intense the media.

Here's an example. A number of years ago, I worked with a company that had a unique service to sell to commercial real estate companies. The service was complex and required some graphics and flow charts to adequately communicate it. So, we created a direct mail piece, sent a certain number of them every day, and called the day we expected the piece to be received in an attempt to talk to the prospect about it when it was in front of him. Today, of course, we'd use a Webinar for the same reasons.

If you have a simple message, like our coffee shop, you can use relatively non-intense media, like a simple road sign. If you have a more sophisticated, complex message, you need to use a medium that delivers that kind of message, like a Webpage, a printed brochure, or a telephone call.

One more principle: You should use the medium that makes the biggest impact for your investment.

You should use the medium that makes the biggest impact for your investment.

As we can see spoken words are the least effective way to communicate. That's why, for example, you can't remember the sermon you heard last Sunday in church. They are convincing at the moment, but easily forgotten.

Images, as in renderings or written words, are more effective than just spoken words, because they will be remembered longer. However, pictures and sound recordings are more effective than renderings.

Seeing the actual product in moving pictures, as in video with sound is more effective than seeing still pictures of the product. Seeing the product is more effective yet, and being able to try it for a while is one of the most effective ways to communicate your presentation.

Again, let's use our coffee shop as an example. We could, I suppose, have you stand out on the sidewalk with a bullhorn and shout your message—"Great Flavor! Low Price! Quick Service!" That would be the least effective way to present your product.

You could print the message on a sign, and that would be more effective, but if you could add a drawing of a steaming hot cup of coffee, it would make the presentation even better. Your next option would be an actual photograph of the cup of coffee.

However, if you could somehow deliver a video of someone pouring the coffee while you verbalized the message, that would be a very effective medium, although it's difficult to envision exactly how that would work. Maybe an animated billboard?

That thought brings us to another principle for choosing the medium through which you present your message. It has to be economically viable. In other words, you probably couldn't sell enough coffee to pay for the cost of an animated billboard.

So although the medium may be more effective, the cost is prohibitive. Better stick with something you can afford.

For our coffee shop, a mobile sign placed at the side of the road would work, as would a simple flier delivered to nearby offices with a photograph of the coffee.

Note: We have assembled a variety of resources to help you accomplish this step of the process. Visit *http://www.sellanythingtoanyone.net/show.php* to review them.

How to Implement the Ideas in This Chapter

1. The more you precisely match the needs of the customer with the specifics of your presentation, the more effective that presentation will be.

2. Remember the difference between features and benefits, and focus on the benefits.

3. Use the four-step process to determine the content of your presentation.

4. Carefully consider the medium for your message.

5. Begin with the written statement of what your customers want, and create a message that precisely matches that statement. Remember: features and benefits.

6. Show your message to some people and get their feedback. Remember, in all of this, more heads will bring better clarity.

7. Once your *message* is ready, decide on the most effective *medium* to deliver that message. Be guided by these criteria:

   ■ The medium should be one with which your customers are currently comfortable.

   ■ The medium should match the message. The more complex the message, the more intense the media.

   ■ Use the medium that makes the biggest impact for your investment.

9

What You Have Is What They Want: One-on-One Selling Situations

In one of my sales training workshops, we were role-playing the presentation part of the sales process. One of the trainees thought that he should thoroughly describe every possible feature of his product line, and methodically droned on and on. The person playing the role of the customer actually began to fall asleep in the middle of the role-play! That was a dramatic example of salespeople getting this wrong.

This is the part of the sales process where you shift gears and gently bring the focus to your solution. Prior to this, the entire focus was on the customer: You selected the right people with whom to engage, you made them comfortable with you, and you found out what they wanted. Now, you want to build on those earlier steps by bringing their focus to your offer. This is where you present what it is you want them to buy.

All of the principles we discussed in the previous chapter apply to one-on-one selling: matching, selecting and prioritizing the features, and turning the features into benefits. However, because you are speaking one-on-one to a human being, the challenges take on some different textures. The challenge here is to match your presentation—not to a segment of customers, but to the needs of this particular human being. No two presentations are exactly alike because, although your offer may be the same, the other half of the equation (your customer), is always different. And no two customers are exactly the same.

Notice that the name of this step of the process is "what you have gives them what they want." There are two parts to this: "what you have," and "what they want." That's a clue to the first principle of one-on-one presenting: Your presentation should be about two things: your offer and the customer. The best one-on-one presentations spend half the time talking about the offer and half the time talking about the customer.

> **Your presentation should be about two things:
> your offer and the customer.**

Remember our discussion of features and benefits from the previous chapter? Features are about your offer, whereas benefits are about your customer. As you prepare and deliver your presentation, keep in mind that roughly half of the words that you say should be words that describe the customer and the impact that your offer will have on him or her.

There are two pieces of a well-done presentation—the preparation and the execution.

Part One: Preparation

Preparation includes these steps:

1. Create the content of the presentation.
2. Create the means to deliver that content.
3. Assemble the communication pieces.
4. Practice the presentation.

Step 1: Create the content of the presentation

If you have done a good job of understanding your customer, you will have a detailed description of what the customer wants, the order of importance of those things, and the personal and emotional issues you must address to communicate effectively with her.

Begin with a disciplined effort to pare down your presentation to those features that most closely match what she wants. There is a natural tendency to want to describe every possible feature of your offer. When you do that, you risk boring the customer and raising issues that are not central to her needs. That can divert her attention to extraneous and potentially negative places. Remember the discussion of multiple features from Chapter 8? That applies directly to presenting one-on-one. Be disciplined and choose to present only those features that directly relate to her wants. If she is interested in other features of your offer, you'll be able to answer questions and toss them in at that time. Start with those issues that are most important to her, and select those features of your product that most directly impact those issues.

Let's illustrate with our freelance grant writer. By methodically working at the previous steps of the process, you would have arrived at an understanding of the needs of a handful of your prospects. You have an appointment to deliver a proposal to one—the executive director of a non-profit organization that assembles and ships medical supplies to areas impacted by natural disasters. In your "find out what they want" stage, you learned that they are pretty good at acquiring private donations in response to various well-publicized disasters, but that those are intermittent and unpredictable. The organization would really like to have a steadier source of income and the board has authorized applications for grants to cover ongoing administrative costs. You are one of several possibilities.

So, you think hard about this situation. What do you have that provides them with what they want? You review your resume and realize that you had successfully acquired a grant for a similar purpose for one of your former employers. You decide to mention that because it reduces the perception of risk—look, you've already successfully done something similar: You've cultured a relationship with a couple of people who are employed by foundations to whom you would apply. That gives you a bit of leg up.

What else do you have that would appeal to him? Of course, you are going to point out your qualifications: educational background, experience, and so on. You can start immediately, without any delay, and that should be a plus.

Finally, you decide on a powerful pricing strategy. You'll defer 30 percent of your fee until, and only if, they get the grant for which you applied. That moves a great deal of the risk from them to you, and makes you partners in the endeavor with them, instead of just a contractor.

So, here's your list of features and benefits:

Feature	Benefit
1. Your background and credentials.	He can feel comfortable that you are capable of doing the job.
2. You have acquired a similar grant for someone else.	He can feel comfortable knowing that you have done this before.
3. You know some people in the foundations to which you'll be applying.	He has a better chance of success.
4. You can start right away.	He can expect money sooner.
5. You'll make 30 percent of your fee conditional upon actually receiving the money.	Reduces his risk, making you the easy decision for him.

Now, let's look at the content of the presentation from the prospect's point of view. You are going to show him that you are capable of the work, you have done this before, you have contacts that improve your chance of success, he can expect money more quickly with you, and you'll share some of his risk.

Congratulations. You've accomplished step one.

Step 2: Create the means to deliver that content

Now that you have decided what to say, you must choose the best way to say it. Here again, we'll combine two of the principles of the previous chapters—knowing your customer and different layers of communication. Ask yourself, "What format or medium would best communicate my message to the customer?"

Are you just going to talk? Or are you going to have pieces of literature to which you refer? Are you going to put everything on a DVD and play it for him? Are you going to create a PowerPoint presentation and project it on his office wall? Be guided by the age and comfort level of the customer, and the levels of effectiveness via the "cone of experience."

Back to our grant writer. Your natural instinct is to prepare a PowerPoint presentation. But, as you think about it, you come to the conclusion that the presentation may make the presentation seem less personal. After all, there is just going to be him and you—you are not presenting to a group. Further, you consider that the grant application, which is your work product, is going to be a document. You decide to use that same format for your presentation, which will further show your capability to effectively communicate with words on paper.

After having made that decision, you review the material in the previous chapter about "levels of effectiveness," and realize that you could add some power to your presentation by adding some photos and actual examples of your work. You go to Facebook, download the photos of your two contacts, and insert them in a page that describes those contacts. Then, you pull up a copy of the successful grant application that you did for a former employer, black out all the identifying information, and print a copy.

You have used the principles in the previous chapter to add some power to your presentation. It's time to move on to step three.

Step 3: Assemble the communication pieces

You have some major decisions behind you. Now, you have to execute them. You create a one-page summary of your presentation with the features and benefits outlined in a very similar fashion to that described previously.

Then, for each of the features, you have another piece of paper, describing the feature in some detail. These are designed to provide more detail and lend credibility to each of your major points. Your credentials are spelled out in detail on one page, for example. On another page, you have the pictures of your current contacts to back up that point. Instead of a separate page to support your assertion that you have successfully done a very similar grant application, you have the copy of the application itself.

As you assemble these pieces of your presentation, you stumble onto a new idea: Proof!

Proof is the specific expression of another powerful principle: It is always more effective to have someone else say something positive about you, than it is for you to do so yourself.

> **It is always more effective to have someone else say something positive about you, than it is for you to do so yourself.**

Proof, then, is the tangible expression of that principle— someone else verifying what you say, or saying something positive about you. Proof can be letters of recommendation, computer reports, articles written about you or your product or company, copies of guarantees or warrantees, independent studies done, and so on.

You realize that although you may have the copy of the grant application that you wrote, it is only your word that it was successful. So, you do a Google search, come up with the press release from your previous employer indicating that they had been awarded the grant, download it, and print it. Proof! You make photocopies of a couple of letters of recommendation, written by former employers—Proof.

With that assembled, you are ready to move to the final step of preparation.

Step 4: Practice

In my first full-time professional selling situation, I sold amplification equipment to classes of hearing-impaired children. The night before every presentation, I rehearsed it. I got the demonstration equipment out, cleaned it off, made sure everything worked, and then I actually rehearsed the presentation, flipping on the switches, into the microphone, and so on.

Of the 29 major purchases made in my territory during the time that I did that, I won 28 of them; even though my product was 30 percent more expensive than the other two competitors (don't ask me about the one that got away).

Practice means just that. Find a private place. Pretend that you are meeting with your prospect. Verbally deliver your presentation using the collateral that you created to support your message. Notice when you stumble across a word, or are tempted to use an awkward phrase. Fix it. Practice again.

I doubt that my practicing the presentation was the only, or even the biggest, reason for that success. Certainly there were additional factors that impacted it, but practicing helped me to do this step better.

And that's an illustration of the formula for success in sales—methodically do each step of the process and do each as well as you can. Have faith that the sum total of your diligent efforts brings success far more often than the shoot-from-the-hip-style of most salespeople.

> **Methodically do each step of the process and do each as well as you can.**

Part Two: Executing the Presentation You Have Prepared

Now you are ready. You've decided on the content, assembled the media, added proof, and rehearsed your presentation. It's time to do it.

Let's remember our fundamental principle for doing this step well: Matching what you have to what the customer wants.

That leads us to an observation that has evolved from decades of selling. You rarely, if ever, really truly understand exactly what the customer wants. You may think you do, and you may have done a superb job of trying to understand the customer, but when all is said and done, you rarely have it completely right.

> **You rarely truly understand exactly what the customer wants.**

One of the places in which this becomes evident is in the presentation. For example, let's say you are our grant writer, in the middle of your presentation, and you've just pointed out that you can start right away, which means that he may not have to wait as long for the money. Your prospect stops you and says, "Oh, that's okay. I'm going on vacation for three weeks, and then I have a major project to attend to when I return. We probably aren't going to want to seriously get into this application for two months."

Oops! That was one of your selling points! You thought it was urgent. It's not. You misunderstood, or just as frequently, something has changed.

Regardless, what you thought was the case, isn't the case. This kind of thing happens so often it becomes the rule, not the exception. That means that you must have some mechanism in place to allow you to become aware of nuances in the prospect's needs, or changes that may have occurred since the last visit.

That mechanism is a mind set and a set of techniques called dialogue. Dialogue is a back and forth conversation. It is not a one-way monologue, whereby you do all the talking. It is a formal, structured way for you to continually elicit the customer's views, thoughts, and feelings in regards to what you are saying.

Begin with the mindset that your presentation should be more like a conversation than a speech. You should be sensitive to the customer's verbal and non-verbal communication, and plan several places in the flow of the presentation to stop and ask for the customer's reaction.

For example, in our grant-writer presentation, after you made your point about having done one just like this for someone else, and while you are showing him the application and the copy of the press release, you could say something like: "Okay?" And then pause to require the customer to respond. Or, you could say, "How important is that to you?"

After you mentioned the two people that you know in the foundation, you could say, "I'm sure you know that provides an advantage." And then be quiet to let the prospect respond to that statement.

Finally, after you mention that you could start anytime, you could say, "So, if you wanted to, we could get started on Monday," and wait for him to respond.

Notice that you planned to draw the customer into the conversation with questions and statements that you phrased in such a way as to elicit the customer's response.

> **The more you can involve the customer in the presentation, the more powerful your presentation.**

Here are three additional tips to help you execute a more effective presentation:

1. **The more you can involve the customer in the presentation, the more powerful your presentation.** Decades ago, as a young salesperson, I was interested in the Dale Carnegie program. A salesperson came to our house, and eventually made a presentation to sign me up for the Dale Carnegie program. He had a little cloth bag in which there were six or eight wooden blocks. On each block was engraved one of the benefits of the Dale Carnegie program: better self-esteem, more confidence, and so on.

   The salesperson spilled the blocks out on the table, and asked me to physically arrange them according to the relative importance I attached to each one. So, for example, "more confidence" might be first, and "better self-esteem next."

I've remembered that presentation for decades. What a great way of getting me physically and emotionally involved in the presentation. That was a great example of this principle.

When I was selling amplification equipment to classrooms of hearing-impaired children, I would put the headset on the teacher, position her at the blackboard, and turn my back and walk away. I would then whisper commands to her into the microphone. All the people in the presentation watched as she wrote the words on the board that I had given her to do. Another real-world example of this principle put in place.

Typically, to work this principle into your presentation requires some creative thought up front in the preparation phase. Ask yourself, "How can I arrange the materials in such a way as to get the customer physically involved in the presentation?"

To the degree that you can, control the environment.

2. **To the degree that you can, control the environment.** The environment has two levels: the macro-environment and the micro-environment. The macro-environment refers to the physical elements surrounding the presentation. For example, if you are presenting to a retail store manager, and you are talking to him or her in the

showroom of the store, that store, including the customers coming in and out, the music in the background, and the other employees all constitute the macro-environment.

If there are sources of interruption, such as customers or the phone, or anything that would draw the customer's attention away from your dialogue with him, then you need to take control of the environment. Ask if you can move to a quieter, more private area. If he says yes, you've added a bit more effectiveness to the presentation. If not, then at least you tried.

The micro-environment refers to the place at which your customer looks during your presentation. As much as you are able, direct your customer's eyes where you want them to be. This is, of course, one of the advantages of using PowerPoint or similar programs to project the content of your presentation, but it doesn't necessarily have to be a technological solution.

For example, at one point in my selling career I sold surgical staplers to surgeons in the operating room suite. I'd often find myself trying to demonstrate the staplers with my briefcase resting on a vacant gurney. Because operating room suites are busy places with lots of activity and distractions, I decided to control the micro-environment in this way: I bought a piece of burnt orange velvet at the fabric store and stored it in my briefcase. When I had an opportunity to present the instruments, I'd first lay the burnt orange velvet down on the gurney, and then set the instruments on top of them. Do you know how compelling and attractive burnt orange is amidst a sea of operating room pastel green and blue? It was almost impossible for the surgeons not to be drawn to the staplers in that micro-environment.

> **Use the customer's language, not your own.**

3. **Use the customer's language, not your own.** There must be something in our DNA that leads us to try to impress the customers with our command of our jargon. We use all these words that have meaning to us internally, but that don't resonate with the customers. That's always a mistake, because it confuses the customer and puts the focus on us, not the customer.

   For example, for eight years, I presented a monthly one-hour telephone seminar to salespeople. Internally, we initially began calling these seminars "virtual seminars." Our files were coded by the number of the seminar, that is, VS-1, VS-25, and so on. When we promoted them to our customers, we called them "TGIF&K seminars"— "Thank Goodness it's Friday and Kahle."

   Our procedure was to post the handouts on the Website, and when someone signed up for the seminar, direct them to download the handouts and connection information. Occasionally someone would have trouble downloading the handouts, and we would have to send them to her as an e-mail attachment. A surprisingly large number of these people claimed to never have received the handouts. Finally, it dawned on us what the problem was. We were calling the handouts "VS-15," our internal language, while the customer was looking for "handouts to the TGIF & K seminar." When we changed the file names to reflect the customer's language and expectations instead of our internal jargon, we solved the problem.

Not only does it eliminate potential misunderstandings, but using the customer's language is a powerful way to connect with the customer, and to make your presentation much more persuasive.

One of my clients had a fastener distribution business. His business was being overrun by the profusion of small orders. They were costly to fulfill and jammed up his system so that he couldn't spend the appropriate amount of time taking care of the larger customers. Here's how he chose to tell me about it: "It's like we are in the middle of a river with all these small orders coming at us, like the flow of the current. We can't seem to make any upstream progress because it's all we can do to tread water and stay afloat."

I said, "It sounds to me like we should build some water sluices and dams to control the flow before it gets to you."

"That's it!" he enthusiastically replied.

I could have used my consultant's jargon to present my solution to him: "Minimum orders, revised policies, training in new procedures, and so on." But they would not have resonated with him. Instead, because he chose to describe his problem like being in the middle of a river, I used that metaphor to describe my solution.

Applying these principles and tips to the preparation and execution of your presentation will enable you to effectively implement this step of the process.

Note: We have assembled a variety of resources to help you accomplish this step of the process. Visit *http://www.sellanythingtoanyone.net/show.php* to review them.

How to Implement the Ideas in This Chapter

- Remember features and benefits. Your presentation should be 50 percent about your offer, and 50 percent about the customer.
- You can't talk about everything, so select those features that most closely match what the customer wants.
- Focus on two steps: Preparation and execution. To prepare your presentation, use the four-step process to prepare the presentation:
    1. Create the content of the presentation.
    2. Create the means to deliver that content.
    3. Assemble the communication pieces.
    4. Practice the presentation.
- To execute the presentation, build in these practices:
    1. Keep in mind that it is a dialogue, not a monologue, and work to draw the customer into the conversation.
    2. As much as possible, control the environment.
    3. Use the customer's language, not your own.

10

Gaining Agreement on the Next Step

Let's review. You have studied your market, identified the right people, and figured out how to interact with them. You've worked at making them comfortable with you, finding out what they wanted, and then you persuasively showed them how what you have gives them what they want.

Now, why did you do all that? I'll bet it is to get an order and to actually sell something. That is, after all, the ultimate purpose of the whole process. That brings us to that point in the sales process that provides us with the definition of success. If you are successful at this point, you have pretty much succeeded at the whole process.

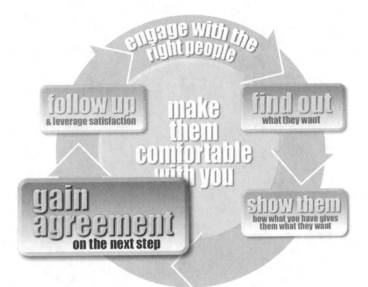

Having said that, closing the sale is by far the most over-hyped phase of selling. If you have the right person, you have uncovered something they want, and you have shown them how what you have gives them what they want, why wouldn't they take the next positive step? It's natural. You just need to help them define what that is, and commit to it.

In mass-selling scenarios, the next step is typically to buy the product. However, in more complex sales, there can be a series of appropriate next steps. They may need to test it, evaluate it, and submit it to a committee.

In this chapter, we're going to examine the principles and practices of actually getting the order in mass-selling situations, and in the next, we'll look at the practices for one-on-one selling.

Let's look at the first principle: Make it easy to buy!

The first principle: Make it easy to buy!

I just returned from our annual vacation in the Caribbean. This year, more than in any other, a number of restaurants refused to take my American Express card. I like American Express and use that card as my first choice wherever I go, but I realize that many of these restaurant proprietors don't want to pay the extra couple of points that American Express charges. In so doing, however, they make it more difficult for me to buy from them. They violated the first rule—they didn't make it easy for me to say yes. In fact, they put some obstacles in the way.

Doesn't it seem obvious that if you want the customer to buy from you, you shouldn't put any obstacles in the way of that? Yet, in the interest of operational efficiencies, countless businesses violate that simple precept.

One of my clients had a long-standing business delivering a commodity product to homeowners. They developed a Website in which they presented all of their offers. When it came time to buy, however, they asked the customer to fill out a credit application rather than buy on a credit card. The credit app would have to be approved; the company would then call the customer, and, on the basis of an approved credit application, allow them to buy. That's another classic example of putting obstacles in the way of doing business. Their Website was not nearly as effective as it could have been, because they didn't make it easy to do business with them.

If you are going to put this principle into play, you must give some thought to implementing the customer's decision to buy, as quickly as he wants to, in almost every way that he wants to buy. If you only take cash, for example, you'll put obstacles in the way of some customers. If you only take credit cards, you'll put obstacles in the way of those who want to pay cash.

Let's apply this principle to our coffee shop and tea-selling Website. At the coffee shop, your business has evolved to the point where you have a drive-up window where you sell the one-dollar coffee product to the commuters, and a traditional service counter inside the store where you take orders for custom-created coffee beverages. You've decided to make it easy for everyone to buy by equipping both stations with card readers and cash drawers. You'll take a credit card, a debit card, and cash for any purchase. You've made it easy for them to give you their money.

On the tea-selling Website, you've come to a similar conclusion, and you are set up to take credit and debit cards, as well as PayPal. You've made the transaction as easy and simple as you can, and you have created a one-click option for returning customers to buy without having to put all their detailed information in each time they order from you.

In addition, you've added three "buy it now" buttons to every product page, and developed an easy option at check out to "shop some more" or "check out now." In doing this you have stumbled on to another simple principle: Give them multiple ways and times to buy. It's a simple idea. The more times you give them the opportunity to buy from you, the more they will take you up on it! So, give them multiple times and ways to buy.

Give them multiple ways and times to buy.

One more principle will help you increase your business. Give them a reason to buy it now.

Give them a reason to buy it now.

The classic reasons to buy it now generally center around two issues—"it is not going to be available long," and/or "the price is going to be higher."

I just watched a Burger King commercial, which is the classic example of "it" not being available much longer. They were promoting a new sandwich, available for a "limited time only." If you want to try this sandwich, you'd better go get it now. If you wait, it won't be available. That's a reason to buy it now.

We can use these principles to increase the business in our coffee shop, as well as the Website. For example, you could buy a special coffee—maybe a special bean or flavor—and make it available for a "limited time only."

Actually, in many cases, you may be able to charge more for it than you do for the regular offering. So, if you sell 12-ounce cups of coffee inside the store for $2.50, you could stimulate additional sales by offering "Special 'till it's gone: Kona coffee from Hawaii $2.75." Not only have you given them a reason to buy it now, you've actually gotten a bit more for it. Creating a daily special—"today only" will convey the same idea.

The same principles can be applied, of course, to our tea-selling website. Those tea cups could be a limited supply, available only for a short time. You could have regular sales where they have to act by a certain time in order to get the best price.

Here's yet one more principle that falls into this category: Encourage them to buy more!

Encourage them to buy more!

When was the last time you ordered a fast-food sandwich, and were not asked, "Would you like fries with your order?" The fast food establishments have mastered this principle. The customer is buying something, and he is in a "yes" frame of mind. Now is the easiest time to increase the size of the sale.

The staff at fast-food restaurants is trained to ask about adding fries. That's one way to encourage their customers to buy more. But that menu sign above the serving counter also conveys the message. Notice all those combinations? If you are in the mood for a burger, why not get the combination? From the business's point of view, it increases the size of the sale by encouraging the customers to buy more.

You can do the same. At the point that the customer is ready to say yes, or maybe already has, suggest something else she could buy. It's incredible how this little principle can add significant dollars to your sales.

When I was a college student, I sold men's suites and sport coats in a relatively expensive men's store to work my way through school. Routinely, when someone had decided to purchase a suit, and we had fitted it to him, he would return to the changing room to slip back into his street clothes. I would take the coat up to the front of the store, select two or three shirts and a sample of ties to go with it. When he came out of the changing room, I'd motion to him to join me at the front of the store, where he could see how good those shirts and ties looked with his new suit. More times than not, they decided to add an additional $50 to the sale by selecting the add-ons.

To apply this principle to your coffee shop, bring in a line of muffins and pastries, and offer a couple of combination deals. "Buy a muffin and a cup of coffee for X." Train your wait staff to ask every time someone buys only coffee, "Would you like a muffin to go with that?" If only one out of 10 say yes, you have significantly increased your sales with no additional sales costs.

Let's consider the tea-selling Website. We could have several combinations: "Four teas from India." "Chinese tea sampler pack," and so on. And at the check out when they are finalizing the order, you could have a little pop-up box say, "Add a unique, custom-crafted tea cup to the order for only $4" with a simple yes or no box to click. Watch how many tea cups you sell, and how you transform the order to a larger size.

Constantly monitor your results.

Chances are you won't be absolutely perfect in crafting your offers every time. Not to worry. By paying close attention, and monitoring your results, you can make a continuous stream of fine-tuning adjustments until you arrive at the right combination of "reasons to buy it now." Think of a mini-process that involves these steps:

Your offer → their response → your analysis of their response → your revised offer.

Keep track of the numbers and percentages. Pay careful attention to the success of your offers to ascertain whether or not they appeal to your customers. For example, to how many customers did your servers say "Would you like a muffin with that coffee for just $6?" Keep track of how many you sell. Analyze it. If you aren't happy with the results, change it.

On your tea-selling Website, if you discover that you made 200 offers of the tea cup for $4, and no one has purchased, it's probably not an attractive offer. Change it.

If your "muffin and coffee" combination doesn't do well, change the offer. If something is working, analyze it to try to figure out what about that makes it desirable, and try to duplicate those principles in an additional offering.

For example, you could discover that your "muffin and coffee" combination at $6 doesn't do well, but, your "Coleen's homemade apple streusel and a cup of coffee for $6.25" sells much better. Maybe, you think, it's the "homemade" that does it. So, you create a revised offer: "Coleen's homemade muffins and a cup of coffee for $6.25" and see how that goes.

By implementing these principles at the crucial point in the sales process where money changes hands, you'll be able to wring the most value out of the entire sales process.

Note: We have assembled a variety of resources to help you accomplish this step of the process. Visit *http://www. sellanythingtoanyone.net/agree.php* to review them.

How to Implement the Ideas in This Chapter

1. Look at your offer, and how you handle the transaction, and analyze it via these criteria:
   - Are you making it easy to buy from you?
   - Are you offering multiple ways and times to buy?
   - Are you, at least on regular occasions, giving them a reason to buy it now?
   - Are you regularly offering them a way to buy more?

2. If you note any weaknesses in your handling of the point of transaction fix them.

3. Set up a system to measure the results of any of-
    fer you make, study the numbers regularly, and
    make modifications as necessary.

11

Gaining Agreement on the Next Step in One-on-One Selling Situations

Ah, this is where it gets a bit dicey. I can't help but think of all the really terrible advice given by sales trainers and writers of "how to close" sales books. "Closing the sale" is the most over-hyped and erroneously taught discipline of all the steps in the process.

Let's begin by looking at the situation from the customer's point of view (always a good idea!). She's the right person, you've made her comfortable with you, you found out what she wanted, and you showed her how what you have gives her what she wanted. If you've done all that well, the decision to buy will be a natural, logical outcome of everything that came before it.

It gets a little sticky when you factor in the customer's buying process. For example, you may be talking face-to-face with an owner of a small business who can very well make the decision to buy right now. The next step in his buying process is to buy. However, you may also be talking to a much larger organization. The person to whom you are talking is the representative of the "new products committee." His next step is to take it to the committee for discussion and resolution.

It would be very appropriate for you to ask the owner for an order, and terribly inappropriate for you to ask the representative of the new products committee for an order. The difference is not you or your offer; it is the customer's buying process.

The first step to gaining agreement on the next step is to understand what the next step is!

The first step to gaining agreement on the next step is to understand what the next step is!

This is broader than just asking for the order at the end of the sales process. It can be applied at every sales interaction along the way.

Every sales interaction has an assumed next step. If you call someone for an appointment, the next step is the appointment. If you present your solution to a decision-maker, the next step is the order. In between, there are thousands of potentially different sales calls, and thousands of potential action steps that follow the sales call.

One of my clients sold production equipment. These were major pieces of machinery that were imported and cost hundreds of thousands of dollars each. We developed a flow chart of the process a buyer goes through to come to a decision to buy this high risk offering. Twenty-eight steps. In other words, if you are the salesperson, you need to ask the buyer, on 28 separate occasions, to take the next step. The final step, to issue the purchase order, was the natural, logical outcome of those 27 steps that came before.

That's a far cry, you are thinking, from my free lance grant writer who just wants to get a project. Not so. Although the applications are a bit different, the underlying principles and processes are the same. By the way, that is, of course, the very rationale of this book. Once you understand the core principles and processes, you can sell anything to anyone anytime.

The underlying process is, on every face-to-face interaction, to put yourself in the shoes of the customer and ask yourself, "If I'm the customer, what is going to be my next step?" Identify that next step, and ask the customer to agree to it. Simple.

As you begin to think about that, it won't be long before you'll stumble onto one of the most powerful rules of this important process step: Always ask for action.

Always ask for action.

Think "A to the third power": **A**lways **A**sk for **A**ction. Exactly what does that mean? Exactly what it says. In every sales interaction, whether it is two minutes on the phone, or two hours in a formal presentation, at the end of that time, ask for action. Always. Everytime. No exceptions.

I know you are thinking, "But I can't gain an agreement every time." That's true, but you sure can try! If you don't try, the agreement will rarely happen on its own.

The agreement is the ultimate rationale for the sales call and the aspect of the interaction that makes it a "sales" call. A sales call is set apart from the rest of the interactions in this world by the fact that it anticipates an agreement.

Without an agreement, the process has been a waste of time. It is the ultimate goal of every salesperson, and of every sales process, and of every sales call.

Notice one more incredibly important thing. When you are asking for action, you are asking for your customer to agree to do something that moves the project forward. The key is that the customer must agree to do something. The action that you are going to ask for is always the customer's action.

Here's an example I often use in my seminars. Let's say you are in a first meeting with a qualified prospect (the right person). After a few minutes' conversation, he says, "I'm somewhat interested in what you offer. I don't have time to talk now. Can you send me some literature?"

You are pleased with that response and you say, "Sure. I'll be back in the office tomorrow and I'll put it in the mail then."

"Okay," he says.

Have you closed that interaction? Have you agreed on the customer's next step? Have you achieved an agreement for action?

Unfortunately, the answer is no to all of those questions. You agreed to do something, but what did the customer agree to do? Nothing.

Let's go back to that scenario and, this time, let's be guided by the rule and Always Ask for Action. The scenario proceeds identically. This time, when he asks if you can send him send literature, you say, "Sure. I'll be back in the office tomorrow and I'll put it in the mail then. You'll probably receive it on Tuesday. How about if I call you on the phone on Wednesday to talk about it and decide where we go from there. Would you have time, at 10 a.m. Wednesday morning, or is the afternoon better?"

He says, "I'm busy Wednesday morning, but I'll talk to you in the afternoon."

"How about 1:30?," you ask.

"Okay," he says.

Have you closed that interaction? Have you agreed on the customer's next step? Have you achieved an agreement for action?

This time, the answer is yes to all three questions. He agreed to talk to you at a specific time. That's an agreement for action. It moves the project forward. Perfect!

I'm sure you can see, at this point, that if you are going to do this well, it will take a little planning on your part. Before every face-to-face interaction, you ought to try to see the situation from the customer's point of view, and attempt to identify his next step. Remember, every face-to-face interaction ought to end in an agreement for action. So, you take a moment and try to identify the action that you'd like to happen.

Then, you create a couple questions that ask for his action. Remember our discussion of asking better sales questions in Chapter 7? All of those principles and processes come into play at this point in the sales process as well.

I'm not going to recreate that chapter here. There is an in-depth discussion of "questions to help you gain agreement" in my book, *Question Your Way to Sales Success*. For now, let me suggest that you create a couple questions that you can use to put the issue on the table and to ask for agreement. If you prepare them before hand, you'll be much more confident in them. And, if your confidence increases, you'll be much more likely to actually use them.

If nothing else, practice this one a few times. It's a generic, all-purpose "agreement identifying" question that is one of my favorites. I use it all of the time: "Where do we go from here?" Or, you can use a variation of it: "What's the next step?"

Notice that this asks the customer to identify the next step. When he does, you simply ask for a date by which that will happen. Bingo. You have an agreement on the next step. It's the lazy man's all-purpose close.

Now, believe it or not, they don't always say yes. It's not at all unusual for them to have some concerns about the decision. Sometimes these concerns are about you and your product, or your price, or some aspect of your offer. But just as commonly, they have concerns about their circumstances, their issues, and their ability to implement this decision.

Let's use our freelance grant writer as an example. This is our second visit with the right person, and you've made your proposal. Remember, your offer was "hire me to write your next grant application." As you think about his next step, you figure that he will either decide to hire you right now, or maybe he'll want to talk the decision over with one of his executives. (That's you thinking about it before the interaction.)

You decide to use this close: "So (customer's name), are you ready to go ahead?" If he is, you'll get the deal right now.

If not, he'll tell you, and you'll have to react accordingly (remember our feedback loop?) You rehearse it a few times so that you are comfortable with it, and off you go to this very important interaction.

When you ask that question, your customer says, "Mmmm. Not quite yet."

Okay, now what? His hesitancy could be grounded in doubts about you. He just doesn't know if you are quite the high-powered grant writer for which he was looking. Or it could be something internal. Maybe this whole process has proceeded much more quickly than he thought it would, and he doesn't have his board's approval on the money yet. Or maybe he's getting ready to take a well-deserved three-week vacation, and he doesn't want to make this decision and then leave for a while. He may have really major issues with one of his departments that is going to require a great deal of his time for the next month or so, and he doesn't want to commit to you when he knows he won't have the time.

I can go on and on with possible scenarios, but you get the idea. There are a countless number of issues on his side that could cause him to hesitate and not agree to the action that you'd like. The point is, you probably don't know what those internal issues are. It could be you, it could be him. So, what do you do now? How about asking! (So much of effective sales practices are just plain common sense!) There's another question that you should have prepared before. The "uncovering concerns" question.

For example, in response to " Not quite yet," say, "Oh?" and then sit quietly while he composes his response to you. Or you could ask something like this: "What concerns do you have?"

It will really help if you understand what his issues are. Sometimes, though not every time, you can do something about them. For example, he might say, "I'm going on vacation for three weeks, and I don't want to get this started until I'm back."

You could come back with something like this: "Good for you. It's great to get away. You know, if you gave me the okay today, I could spend the time researching the issue, and when you got back, we'd be ready to move ahead. In fact, that would be one less thing for you to think about on vacation, and one less thing to deal with when you come back." (Remember features and benefits from Chapter 8. You've just given him a couple of benefits.)

If you had never uncovered his concern, you would have never been able to offer a different way to look at it. There are no guarantees. Just because you responded well to his concern doesn't mean that he's ready to say yes, but, you have improved your chances. He is more likely to say yes after your comment than before. So much of sales success lies in these kinds of small margins. If you can do that almost every time, you'll gain a significantly greater number of yes's than if you did not. It is in these small things that the great salespeople distinguish themselves from the mediocre.

What if the issue is not something internal to him, but it is you? What then? Follow the same plan and ask. Just understand that he is not likely to be as forthcoming, unless he is a completely insensitive clod. He's not likely to say, for example, "I don't think you are qualified." Instead, he'll make up something, such as "I want to think about it," or, "There are a few other people who I'm talking to."

What do you do? If you are really sure of yourself, do exactly the same thing I recommended previously and give him a non-threatening, open-ended question. React and respond to what he says.

If you can't see yourself hanging in there to that degree, then just repeat the key pieces of your proposal and the benefits to him, and ask for a certain date and an appointment to resolve the issue. If you walk out of there with an appointment to bring the thing to closure, you will have done well.

It is better to react and respond to what he says. He may say, for example, "That's more than what I had anticipated spending" (the classic price objection). Or he could pick out anything from your offer and react negatively toward it. In either case, your most effective strategy is to either minimize his concern, or maximize your benefits.

"Minimize" means to help him see that his concern is really minor in light of everything that he's getting when he does business with you. You could say, for example, "I realize that this may be more than what you were expecting to pay. Let's say it is $1,000 more. When you compare that with the target of $250,000 we want to bring in with this grant, it is really nothing—less than 1 percent. That's probably not worth the wait."

You made his issue seem small in comparison with what he may potentially get.

You can also do exactly the opposite. Maximize your benefits relative to his concern. In the same situation, you could say something such as this: "I realize that it may be more than what you were expecting to pay. When you think about what the potential pay-off is—$250,000 in new money, a new project begun, a number of people benefited by it, an additional employee—it really makes it seem worth it."

This time, you have maximized your benefits. Minimize and maximize are easy to remember, and simple and easy ways to respond to his concerns—particularly when they have to do with you and your offer.

There is one last piece of this puzzle. Let's go back to our original process diagram. Notice again that "Making them comfortable with you" is not a sequential step in the process; it's an ongoing exercise that touches everything that you do. It's particularly important to keep it on top of your mind at this point in the process. Notice something about the sales process. Up until this point, it has revolved around exchanging information—a relatively non-intense interchange. In other words, you've asked for information (what he wants) and he's given it to you. You have provided him with information (how what you have gives him what he wants), and he's considered it. That's a relatively non-threatening communication interchange.

Now, however, there is a different dynamic. You are asking for action. That's commitment—not just information exchange. It's not unusual for the atmosphere to get a little tense. That's particularly true if he hasn't said yes. He's taken the position that he is not ready to say yes. He's verbalized that, and now he has some ego invested in that position. You hold a different position. So to some degree you are at odds with each other. If he changes his mind, he has to back down from a verbalized position. This can be tense.

That's why you need to pay particular attention to him being comfortable with you. At this point in the process it is so easy to allow the tension to eclipse and submerge the comfort level. All the hard work that you have done can evaporate in a moment of tension.

I recommend to salespeople in my seminars that they go so far as to "finesse" the customer before they deal with the content of what the customer said. In other words, they do some things to dissipate the tension before they react to the customer's words.

Specifically, I teach them to empathize, probe, and clarify before they respond to the content in the customer's words.

"Empathize" means that you express to the customer that you understand what he is saying, thinking, or feeling, and that you give him a reason to believe you. For example, you could say, "I understand how you feel. It does seem like a lot of money doesn't it? A couple of my other clients had the same response initially."

When you empathize and give him a reason to believe you, you release a lot of the tension that has seeped into the situation. It's like when you blow a balloon up to the point where it is about ready to burst. It will just take a little more pressure to blow it apart. Then, you open the bottom and let some of that high-pressure air escape. The tension comes out of the balloon, and it is more manageable. That's what you do when you empathize with the customer.

Next, you should probe. That means to follow your empathizing comment with an open-ended non-threatening inquiry. Something such as, "Help me understand. When you say that it is more than you were expecting, what exactly does that mean?"

Maybe the customer responds with a comment like this: "I had budgeted $5,000 for this, and your proposal is for $6,000."

Great. Now you know. So you clarify and verify and say: "Okay, so, what you are saying is that my proposal is $1,000 more than you had budgeted. Is that right?"

He says, "Yes." And now that you have released the tension, got him talking, clarified the issue, and got him to agree with you; now you can respond to the issue.

That whole process of "finessing the customer" is a higher level sales skill, and only for you if you are confident and competent in your ability to pull it off.

Note: We have assembled a variety of resources to help you accomplish this step of the process. Visit *http://www. sellanythingtoanyone.net/agree.php* to review them.

How to Implement the Ideas in This Chapter

- Gaining agreement is the natural expected outcome of every sales interaction.
- It always involves an agreement on the part of the customer to do something that moves the project forward, buying being just one of a series of possible next steps.
- To effectively implement this step of the process: Identify the expected next step in every sales interaction before the interaction.
  1. Prepare a question or two and practice them.
  2. Expect that there will be some concerns, and ask about them.
  3. Think in terms of minimizing and maximizing any concerns that you are not able to do anything about.
  4. Focus on keeping them comfortable with you, especially at this stage of the process.

12

Follow Up and Leverage Satisfaction

Wait! You are not finished yet. Not if you want to do this sales thing well, that is.

You should feel pretty good about yourself at this point. You have, with thoughtfulness and discipline, successfully worked through the first five stages of the sales process. You have identified the right people, engaged with them, made them comfortable with you, found out what they want, showed them how what you have gives them what they want, and came to an agreement with them. There's probably some new money in the till to confirm your success.

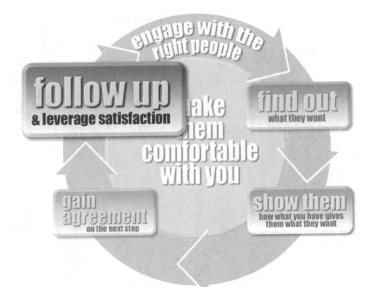

But the most money, and the greatest fulfillment, is yet to come. What if you could add just one more step to the process and, as a result, create not just a customer, but a relationship? And what if you could create that relationship with this customer where you were always their first choice, they preferred you and your offering no matter what other offers were presented to them, they came back over and over again, and spent money with you? Maybe they would even tell their family and friends about you, and those folks would come to you ready to buy. The relationship with the customer would be like an annuity, almost automatically depositing cash in your account regularly for the foreseeable future. Would life be good, or what?

It would be good for a number of reasons. First, the second, third, fourth, and fifth sales, and all those that happen after the first purchase, are the easiest sales for you to achieve.

You know how hard you worked to bring that customer to the point where he gave you money for what you have. Now, he comes back and does it again, with almost no additional effort on your part. If you can keep that customer coming back, it makes all of your previous efforts so much more effective. Think of your return on sales time and effort invested. The returning customer is where you make your money.

> **The returning customer is where you make your money.**

It is, in fact, the easiest of all sales situations. Here's another one of those spectrums, comparing different kinds of selling situations:

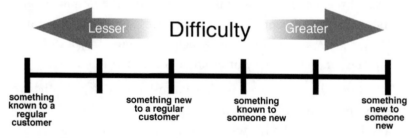

Notice that the situation on the far left, the easiest sale to make, is selling something known to someone who has already bought from you. That's what we are talking about here.

The next easiest sale to make is to sell something new to people who have previously bought from you. Because they already know you and trust you, dealing with you on something additional is much less risk for them. It's easy and comfortable to buy from you. When you develop relationships with your customers, those relationships provide an opportunity to grow your business.

The next easiest sale to make is to sell something known to people who are new to you. An example of this occurs when that customer walks into your coffee shop for the first time, and buys a cup of coffee from you. They know coffee, but until they tasted that first cup, they didn't know your coffee.

The most difficult sale to make is to sell something new to people who are new to you.

Let me use our coffee shop and tea-selling Website to illustrate. In both of those cases, you have been operating at level three. People know what coffee is, and they know what tea is. For 99 percent of your market, it is something known. Now, they may not know the exact differences in your offer, but the general category of product is a known quantity.

If you were to have developed a unique, totally new beverage made out of the refined sap of the pine tree, for example, you would have something totally new to try to sell to people who didn't know you. That would be level four. That's pretty tough to do.

So, most of our time in this book has been devoted to coaching you through a level three situation.

Let's go up to level two, which is something new to people who have purchased from you. This is what you do when you decide to offer hot spiced cider as well as coffee to your $1 customers. Something new. Better yet, you offer a small package of three pieces of mint candy they can use as an afternoon pick-me-up. You don't advertise them, you just offer them for an additional $.50 to your drive-up customers.

I predict that you are going to sell lots of them, because they already know and trust you, and it's an easy transfer of trust to try this new thing. (Remember our discussion of risk in an earlier chapter? With your new offering you are a lower risk because of the relationship.)

But the easiest sale to make is the second, third, and forever-after sale of the one-dollar cup of coffee to the person who tried it the first time.

I must confess a certain laziness and interest about the short cut in my character. I recall certain high school teachers being frustrated with my constant search for the better, easier way to do things. Unfortunately, or maybe fortunately, I have never seen a reason to do things the hard way when an easier and simpler approach could be identified with just a little bit of thinking. That applies to the world of selling. Selling more to the returning customer is the easiest of all sales to make. Why not spend just a little bit of time and effort trying to make that happen?

While it is, from a cold-blooded financial perspective, always smarter to entice the customer to come back, there is an additional benefit. Some of these people will come into your coffee shop so often that you come to know them, and they you. You really do create relationships with some of these folks. And for most of us those relationships are fulfilling, satisfying, fun, and one of the fringe benefits to being competent at selling. Although it is primarily about the money, it is not all about the money.

> **While it is primarily about the money,
> it is not all about the money.**

That's why this final step of the sales process is so productive. In the next chapter, we'll talk about how to do this well in a one-on-one selling situation. In this chapter, we are focusing on the "mass" selling situations, typified by our coffee shop and Website.

Notice the first phrase describing this step is "follow up." That means that you inquire how satisfied the customer was with his purchase. In an ideal world, you would have a conversation with every customer as they sipped their latte. In the real world, it means that you have surveys available, hard copy for the coffee shop, electronic for the Website, and that you encourage people to respond. You hope to get enough of them back to learn something about how your customers think and feel about you and your offer. (There's that feedback loop again.)

You can do this yourself if you have a tight budget. Or you can hire a local professional or a Web-based company to help you. It should take you about 30 seconds to Google "customer satisfaction surveys," and come up with a dozen prospective vendors.

The point is that you never cease to inquire. Something is always changing—either your product, your service, or your customers. You need to keep that feedback loop churning so that you are aware, as soon as possible, of changes that will impact you.

The second word in the description of this step is "leverage." Used in this context, it means to use something to provide something else. Just like when you borrow money and then invest it, you leverage someone else's money into more for you. In this case, you turn their satisfaction with your product or service into additional revenue for you. The way you do that is to give them a reason to come back over and over again.

> **Give them a reason to come back over and over again.**

Yesterday I stopped in to the local Walgreens for some travel-sized toothpaste. When I got my purchase home, I noticed on the back of the receipt a coupon for three dollars off on my next purchase. Providing, of course, that I bought a certain amount, and by a certain date. That's a reason to come back.

I used to have an office in downtown Grand Rapids. Directly below my office, on the first floor of the building, was a coffee shop. I was a frequent customer. I had, of course, a card on which there were seven little cups of coffee illustrated. Each time I bought a cup, they would punch the card, and when all the little cups were punched out, I'd get a free cup. There were so many frequent customers like me, that the coffee shop created a little card file, and would keep our cards on file so that we didn't have to carry them around. They would look in the "K" section, retrieve my card, punch it, and put it back in the card file. That specter of a free cup of coffee incented me to keep coming back.

I'm an "Elite" level customer with Continental Airlines. I got there by flying a lot of miles on their airline. That means that I get to board the plane before the mass of passengers get upgraded to first class at no cost, and my bags come off the line before everyone else's. That may not sound like a big deal, but to a frequent flier those are valuable perks. It keeps me coming back. Because I have to qualify every year, I encourage my travel agent to book me on Continental. The idea of a "status" that brings a grab bag of perks with it is a reason to come back.

An interesting aside to my Elite status with Continental is that it puts me on an e-mail list. I probably get some kind of offer from them every week. That's a great example of another principle: make multiple offers.

Make multiple offers.

That means that, once you have customers, you regularly offer them something additional to buy. Remember: They like you, they trust you, and they have taken a risk with you. It's just natural that they would look positively on offers to buy additional products and services from you.

If it is your coffee shop, for example, you could do what every fast food restaurant in the world does by asking at the point of purchase if they'd like something else. Not just something else in general, but a very specific item. So, your servers could say, "Would you like one of these warm, fresh-baked oatmeal raisin cookies with your coffee?" Here are some ideas:

- You could hand each person a little coupon for 15 percent off the oatmeal raisin cookie the next time they are in your shop.
- You could get their e-mail address, and e-mail them a special deal every other week.

- You could collect their address and mail them a post card with a special coupon every other week.

Once you have the concept, there are an unlimited number of possibilities for your application of that concept.

Once you get a good number of your customers coming back on a regular basis and buying more of what they bought the first time you will be incredibly successful.

Sometimes, the results are so great that you can relax your customer-acquisition efforts, and, for a while enjoy the fruits of your labors. When you are good at selling, life truly is sweet.

Note: We have assembled a variety of resources to help you accomplish this step of the process. Visit *http://www. sellanythingtoanyone.net/follow.php* to review them.

How to Implement the Ideas in This Chapter

1. Think about what you can do, in addition to providing a quality product for the price, to entice a customer to come back again. Specifically, consider:
   - Continuity programs, such as buy seven cups and get the eighth cup free.
   - Discounts and coupons for return customers.
   - Special perks and services for returning customers.

2. Regularly make multiple offers to your best customers.

13

Follow Up and Leverage Satisfaction in One-on-One Selling Situations

So, you have created a customer, you've actually sold something, and you have some money in the bank. Feel free to celebrate and luxuriate in the good feelings that bubble out of you. That's one of the fringe benefits to selling—it feels great when you succeed.

Before you become too enraptured with yourself, let me remind that you are not finished. There is a greater goal, and a larger and more encompassing strategy into which this transaction fits. If you focus all of your time and energy on creating sales, you will, unfortunately, miss the mark.

In a very fundamental sense, in face-to-face, one-on-one selling, the ultimate goal is something larger and more significant than the sale itself. It is the creation of a positive business relationship, because the relationship supersedes the transaction and makes all future transactions much easier and more profitable. Think of that annuity.

For example, if you have a great experience with the place from which you bought your TV, you are much more likely to go back there again. The next time, you are inclined to buy from them, less likely to price shop, and more likely to be less critical and demanding. You may even tell your friends about that place.

From the seller's point of view, he has succeeded in creating a relationship with you because you are favorably inclined to come back, buy again, and refer your friends. The second sale is so much easier than the first, because now you are less risk to the buyer. That's the net result of a positive business relationship.

And the ultimate positive business relationship is something I call a "partner." A partner is someone who trusts you, believes you consistently bring value to him, sees you and your company as an integral part of his business, and buys almost everything he can from you.

The following illustration depicts a different way of looking at your fundamental strategy as a one-on-one, face-to-face salesperson.

The Fundamental Sales Strategy

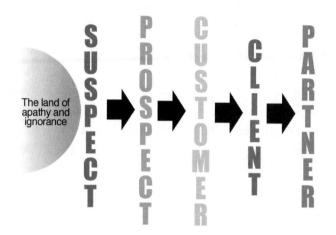

Your fundamental, long-term strategy is to develop and nurture a passel of partners. Your partners then become an asset to your organization, providing years of revenue, in the same way that a brand or product line is an asset to the company. You can't note them on your balance sheet, but they are, nevertheless, one of the sources of future wealth for both you and your company.

Notice in the illustration that your fundamental strategy begins with the land of apathy and ignorance, in which your suspects live. They don't know who you are, and they don't care. Your job, which we discussed in the chapters on "engaging with the right people," is to reach into the land of apathy and ignorance and identify people who you suspect might one day do business with you. Then you learn something about them, and eliminate those who aren't really prospects to focus on those who are prospects. With those who are prospects, you engage with them, make them comfortable with you, find out what they want, show them how what you have gives them what they want, gain an agreement on the next step, and BINGO, you have a sale! You have created a customer.

Now, notice the next two steps in the process. When a customer buys over and over from you, he becomes a "client." And some clients will be so enamored by the value of what you bring and the ease of doing business with you that they will commit to do a lot of business with you. They become partners.

The process of moving customers to clients and clients to partners throws off money, almost as a fringe benefit. Before they can become partners, they have to become clients. And in order to move from being a customer (someone who buys from you once) to clients, they have to believe that you bring them value and can meet their needs on an on-going basis.

One of the most powerful one-on-one sales calls you can make is what I call the ROF call. That stands for "Relationship building, Opportunity identifying, Follow up." It's the sales call you make after the customer has purchased and implemented your offer. For the realtor, it's the call you make on your buyers after they have moved into their new home. For the car salesperson, it's the phone call after the customer has driven off the lot with the new car. For the B2B salesperson, it's the visit you make after they have begun to use your new service or product. And for our freelance grant writer, it is the visit you arrange after the grant application has been submitted.

Why would you do it? After all, you've made the sale, because you understand the bigger picture. It's not just about this sale; it's about the relationship.

> **It is not just about this sale; it's about the relationship.**

It's powerful because it's unusual. When was the last time you had a salesperson contact you after the purchase? Because you will be one of the very few salespeople who actually care enough to follow up after the sale, you will stand out, head and shoulders, above your competitors.

Here's an example. Fifteen years ago, I needed to hold a small meeting with about eight of my customers. I rented a small conference room for a couple hours in a local hotel. No meals or rooms involved. Just a small conference room. I think it cost $25. It was probably the smallest sale that the meetings department of that hotel could make. Two days after the meeting, I received a phone call from the salesperson who rented the room to me.

"Was everything satisfactory?" she wanted to know. "Was the room clean, the temperature okay?"

I was so impressed by the fact that she cared enough to call that I recommended that hotel consistently, and used it for every local meeting I held for the next 15 years.

The ROF call is powerful for one more, very specific and tangible reason. It often produces additional opportunities. At the end of this very specific sales call, you ask for other opportunities.

Here's how you do it. After you have delivered what they purchased from you, then call them for an appointment. When you are one-on-one with them, first ask about their satisfaction with what they bought. At this point, either of one or two things will happen. They will indicate they are satisfied or they weren't. If they weren't, you need to apologize and do whatever you can to fix it. It's good that you found out right now, before it has a chance to fester and spread to other potential customers.

If they are satisfied, great. Confirm it. Then ask them what other opportunities they have for you and your service or product in the near future. If they indicate something, good for you, you have an additional opportunity to work on. (You have "found out what they want" again.) If they don't, it's okay.

Now, you want to probe for external opportunities. These are potential relationships and opportunities for you outside of the confines of this customer's reach. Does he know other people to whom he can refer you? In a large organization, it could be other departments or plants. In a smaller one, it could be business colleagues. For an individual, it could be friends and neighbors.

If they provide you with a name or two, you now have a shortcut into an engagement with a "right person." And you are back at the start of the sales process with someone else. Because you have a recommendation from a trusted reference, you are entering that engagement with an advantage.

So, you have made an ROF call and wrung additional value out of the transaction. But what if they have no near-term additional opportunities? How do you develop a positive business relationship with this customer when there is no reasonable expectation of additional business in the short-term?

Think in terms of "top of mind awareness." This is known in the advertising world as TOMA. TOMA means that you work to keep your name, or your company's name, or your products, on the customer's mind, so that, when the time comes for him to buy again, he first thinks of you.

Now, think in terms of "touches." Touches are light, non-intensive communications from or about you to your customers that spotlight your name, and keep you at the top of their lists.

Now, put those two concepts together—TOMA touches. That's the answer to the question, "How do you develop a positive business relationship with this customer when there is no reasonable expectation of near term business?"

Keep your name in front of them with TOMA touches.

TOMA touches are all around us. When you receive that birthday card from your life insurance agent, that's a TOMA touch. When you receive that quarterly newsletter from the realtor who helped you buy or sell your last home, that's a TOMA touch. Those emails from that investment newsletter you signed up for? A TOMA touch. That calendar that was mailed to you by your auto insurance company? A TOMA touch.

Notice that they all have some common elements. They are personal, addressed to you by name. They carry the name and contact information of the seller, they reflect positively on him or her, and they are light and non-intrusive.

In the B2B world, TOMA touches can be creative. They can range from a fun exhibit at the trade show or convention, to the gift basket delivered at Christmas.

Anything you can do to make your touch stand out and get noticed will be worthwhile. For example, in my world where all my client's vendors send Christmas cards, I send Thanksgiving cards. (Now don't everybody go out and do this!) Instead of being buried in the pack of Christmas cards, because mine is unusual, it stands out.

For years I called on hospitals. It was a common practice for many of the vendors to bring in Christmas gift baskets. I arranged with my wife, who is a gourmet cook, to create a large variety of home-made cookies and candies. We'd package them in disposable water carafes and bed pans, wrap them in colored cellophane, and take them to my customers. Believe me, everyone else's gift basket looked like a third-string bench player compared to my superstar TOMA touch.

The possibilities for TOMA touches are endless. Think in terms of all the electronic communications possible: Twitter, LinkedIn, e-mail, and so on. Then think about hard-copy touches, such as calendars, imprinted pens, and self-stick note pads with your name on them. There are entire catalogs brimming over with these kinds of possibilities. And don't forget personalized birthday and holiday cards.

Explore more extensive and expensive possibilities as well. Remember my bed pans packed with homemade candies and cookies. Consider, if it is appropriate for your business, joining organizations to which your customers belong.

The trade associations and Rotary clubs all provide you an opportunity to keep your name at the front of their minds by mingling with them live and in person.

Finally, if the amount of potential revenue is large enough, consider strategically entertaining your highest-potential customers.

> **If the amount of potential revenue is large enough, consider strategically entertaining your highest-potential customers.**

Consider this experience of mine from my days of selling for a wholesale distributor. I had a high-potential account that did not respond to my efforts. Months went by and I couldn't get anywhere in this huge account.

My company owned four season tickets to the University of Michigan football games, and it was my turn to use them. I invited the head of the purchasing department from that account and her spouse to join my wife and I. We spent the afternoon together, first enjoying a traditional tailgate meal, and then a great college football game.

Immediately thereafter, however, I began to do business in that account. Business grew continually until it eventually became my largest account. The football game was the turning point in the relationship.

It wasn't that I gained "inside" information. We didn't even talk about business. But my customer came to know me better, and, in so doing, became more comfortable with me as a person. And that made all the difference.

That was not the first nor the last time for that experience. I regularly treated two of my customers with their spouses to join my wife and I for a dinner at Greek Town in Detroit, followed by a Tiger's game. We never talked business, but afterward, business always grew. Again, it wasn't that we exchanged business information, cut deals, or anything of that nature. What did happen, every time, was that my customers came to know me better and differently. We became friends instead of just buyers and sellers.

There is an important truth illustrated by these examples. People like to do business with people they know. The better they know you, the more likely it is that they'll do business with you. When they spend time with you outside of the business setting, they come to know you better. It really is that simple.

Now, this doesn't mean that you can charge 20 percent more than your competitors, nor does it mean that you can sell an inferior product, or that your company can get away with second-class service. But when many of these things are viewed by the customer as the same as what your competition offers, you are more likely to get the business if you are the one who has the greater relationship with the customer. The relationship doesn't stand in place of quality, price, and service, but it can provide a competitive edge.

In my seminars, I liken the role of the relationship in selling to an oil can that is used to lubricate the gears of a sophisticated machine. If you stop oiling the gears, eventually the machinery is going to break down. The oil lubricates the interaction, and makes everything work smoother. Building powerful personal relationships with your customers is like oiling the gears. It just makes everything move that much smoother and easier. It is possible to sell without good relationships with your customers, but it is much harder.

In this time of high-tech communication, powerful personal relationships provide the high-touch for which many people are subconsciously hungering. Robert Putnam, in his landmark book, *Bowling Alone*, quoted a study by an MIT researcher that concludes:

> "Though some unimportant business relationships and casual social relationships will be established and maintained on a purely virtual basis, physical proximity will be needed to cement and reinforce the more important professional and social encounters."

Later, more directly to our point, the research concludes:

> "Widespread use of computer-mediated communication will actually require more frequent face-to-face encounters, and extensive deep, robust, social infrastructure of relationships must exist so that those using the electronic media will truly understand what others are communicating to them."

In other words, even in this high-tech world characterized by voice mail, e-commerce, and instant messaging, face-to-face relationships are necessary.

Is there, then, a place for entertaining your customers in this high tech sales environment? Absolutely! *The question becomes not whether or not you ought to, but how to do it in such a way as to gain the greatest benefit.* Here are some thoughts on how to entertain effectively.

Entertaining Strategically

Having lunch every Tuesday with your buddy who happens to work for one of your customers is not entertaining strategically. That's a waste of sales time. Instead, make a list of all the individuals who could be instrumental in buying your products and services. Rank them in order of importance using criteria, such as how important they are to the sale, and how much business they control.

Then, start at the top and methodically work down through the list. Try to spend social time—not business time—with each. I have found evening or Saturday afternoon events work best. Sports events, concerts, and plays are excellent because they are attractive and appealing to a lot of people. To sit at the 40-yard line of a University of Michigan football game, for example, is probably a once-in-a-lifetime experience for most people.

Remember: The purpose is to get to know one another better as people—not as buyer and seller. So, don't talk business unless your customer brings it up. And no sales pitches, please. When you do that, you harden the buyer/seller roles that each of you play. That's exactly the opposite of what you want to have happen. Instead, search for personal common ground—things that you have in common with your customer. You are trying to get to know each other as people, not as role-players.

I've found it to be more effective to invite the customer and his or her spouse or boyfriend or girlfriend to join my wife and me. Having the other two people makes the customer feel more at ease, and increases the likelihood that it will be a pleasant social evening.

When you are entertaining, remember that you are host and that you should attend to all the details. That means that you make the dinner reservations, and you see to the parking and transportation. If you are at a sporting event, you have cash to pay for beer and hot dogs. Think the evening through in detail, and prepare for all the contingencies.

And while a beer or two is okay, be careful with your use and provision of alcohol. Too much alcohol can leave a literal, as well as figurative, bad taste in your customer's mouth.

Finally, don't allow the evening to go to extremes in any way. Don't be the loudest fan, nor the last to leave. Don't order the most or the least expensive item on the menu. Be gracious and moderate in everything you do.

Strategic entertaining can be one of your most powerful strategies. It is a way to build relationships that provide you with a competitive edge, while at the same time meeting the customer's preference to do business with people he or she knows.

When you have created a passel of partners, and have developed positive business relationships with lots of your customers, you have arrived at the end game for a salesperson. It's all easier from here.

Note: We have assembled a variety of resources to help you accomplish this step of the process. Visit *http://www. sellanythingtoanyone.net/follow.php* to review them.

How to Implement the Ideas in This Chapter

1. Make an ROF call on every customer, regardless of how large of a purchase they made.

2. Strategically entertain your highest-potential customers.
3. Make a list, in order of potential, of the highest potential individuals.
4. Create opportunities to spend time with them outside of the office.

14

What's Next?

It shouldn't take you long to realize that, although the sales process is a step-by-step set of practices, you don't actually do just one thing at a time. Rather, you are continually engaged in different steps with different people all the time.

In the coffee shop, for example, you don't just entice those local office workers to come in one week, and then the next week find out what they want, and then the next week entice them with a persuasive offer. Although it works that way with one person, the reality is that you have multiple people, all at different stages with you, at the same time. So, every day you have some people who you are attracting into the shop for the first time, others to whom are you are making a persuasive offer, and others with whom you are following up and trying to turn into relationships.

Your next challenge, then, is to orchestrate a way that you can do all these things, simultaneously, but with a constantly evolving set of customers. Every day of every week you'll want to:

- Engage with the right people.
- Make them comfortable with you.
- Find out what they want.
- Show them how what you have gives them what they want.
- Gain an agreement for the next step.
- Follow up and leverage satisfaction.

Your job is to manage a set of processes, making sure that you are doing enough of the right things, and doing each of these as well as you can. In order to do that, you'll need to see your sales process as a system.

> **Your job is to manage a set of processes, making sure that you are doing enough of the right things, and doing each of these as well as you can. In order to do that, you'll need to see your sales process as a system.**

Every complex, repeatable human work eventually becomes systematized. Mechanics use a system to diagnose the problem with your car, as do doctors to uncover the cause of your complaint. Your lawn maintenance people do their work systematically, as does the lawyer who represented you, the teachers who taught you, and the hair stylist who does your hair. Your sales system is no exception. The Encarta dictionary defines a system as: "A combination of related parts organized into a complex whole...a method or set of procedures for achieving something."

If you are going to sell to a number of people, then you'll need to begin to think of your selling process as a system.

For example, think of the system that is necessary for a factory to produce something like a plastic dinner plate. The system consists of "inputs," or the plastic sheets that are the raw material for the plates. Then there are "processes" that are applied to the raw material that cut and shape, smooth, polish, and package those plates. Finally, the system consists of the "outputs," or the finished boxes of plastic plates, that are put on the trucks and shipped off to their buyers.

Your selling system consists of "inputs"—the suspects and prospects that are the starting point of your system. As you move them through your system, you apply certain "processes"— the steps of the sales process. What comes out of your system are dollars of revenue and, eventually, "partners."

If you were in charge of that dinner plate factory, you'd want to measure how efficient and effective your system was, and you would make regular refinements to the system.

It's the same thing with you. You are in charge of your selling system. Therefore, if you are going to do it better, you'll need to measure various aspects of it, and make regular refinements to the system. At various places earlier in this book, we've talked about measuring certain specific processes. Now, we're going to take that concept and apply it systematically.

You do that by first measuring and then refining the quantity and quality of key activities.

> **The issue now is managing the quantity and quality of key activities.**

Let's define some terms: Key activities are those things that you do—events that you create—that are essential to the successful completion of the sales process. Let's say you could break your sales process down into no more than seven specific events that must take place in order for you to be successful.

In your coffee shop, for example, you might list these:

- Come into the store, or approach the drive up window.
- Order their first cup of coffee
- Come back more than once
- Order something in addition to coffee
- Provide us with their name and e-mail address.

If you are the freelancer involved in a one-on-one selling situation, you might list these:

- Accept a phone call from me and agree to an appointment.
- Articulate the need for additional funds.
- Agree to accept a proposal.
- Accept a proposal.
- Sign a contract.

Let's note some things about these key activities. Notice that these events are not exactly the same thing as our sales process. When you understand the sales process, and apply it to your specific situation, you then create specific expressions of that process that are unique to your selling situation. Thus, "agree on the next step" may mean "order their first cup of coffee" at the coffee shop, and "sign a contract" for the freelancer. Think of the events as objective verification that you have accomplished a step in the process.

Some of the process steps are difficult to verify. For example, how do you know when you have "made them comfortable with you"? Or when have you sufficiently "found out what they want"? In their purest expression, these two represent unattainable ends. Are your customers ever really totally comfortable with you? When have you uncovered every last bit of their constantly changing and evolving needs and wants?

Even though it may be difficult to verify that you have successfully completed a process step, that doesn't make it any less important. The way to deal with this conflict between the ideal and the real is to create measurable events that seem to indicate that you have, at least to some degree, accomplished a necessary step in the process.

So, you look at each step of the process and ask, "What event would indicate the likelihood that we had accomplished that step of the process?" The answers you come up with are in the list of key activities.

Notice one more thing. Key activities must be measurable. They have to describe events that we can easily and fairly measure. So, "making them comfortable with us" is not measurable. But, "coming into the coffee shop," which would probably not happen unless they were somewhat comfortable, is measurable.

Notice also that each of the key activities is expressed in terms of what the prospect/customer does. It's not what you do, it is what they do.

Now, if we are going to ensure our success at sales, we have to sell more than one person. We have to sell a sufficient quantity of people to make all this time and effort worthwhile. So, for example, if we do everything perfectly, and only sell one cup of coffee per day, we are not going to be in business for too many more days.

That means you have to do enough of the right things— the key activities. Because you have to do enough of them, you need some way to measure them. Let's look at each key activity listed and figure out a way to measure them.

1. **Come into the store, or approach the drive-up window.** We could come up with a low-tech approach of having a small pad of paper and charging one employee with the project of creating a hash mark every time someone walked into the store or approached the drive-up window.

   There may be a high-tech solution of putting a sensor and automatic counter at both locations, and letting the technology do it.

2. **Order their first cup of coffee.** Someone is going to have to ask "Is this your first time here?" when the customer orders coffee. If the answer is yes, let's use the hash mark approach again. Or maybe we could use a special code on the cash register. So, item 001 is a cup of coffee for a first-timer, while item 002 is that same cup of coffee, this time purchased by a returning customer.

3. **Come back more than once.** If the answer is "no" to the previous question, the hash mark could go in a different column, or the waiter could be trained to use a different product code.
4. **Order something in addition to coffee.** Easy enough. We'll just count up the number of sales that incorporate coffee and at least one more thing at the end of every day.
5. **Provide us with their name and e-mail address.** We want this so that we can e-mail them occasionally, make "multiple offers" to them, and gradually build a relationship with them. This also is easy to measure. Just count up the number of names on the list at the end of every day or week.

Let's do the same with the one-on-one key activities:

1. **Take a phone call from me and agree to an appointment.** There's our hash mark system again.
2. **Articulate the need for additional funds.** A bit more difficult. Suppose we create a form with three questions on it.
    1. "To what degree is your current budget sufficient for everything you want to do?"
    2. "What sort of consequences will there be, if you don't find additional funds?"
    3. "How much additional funding would you like to have this year?"

    When you recorded their answer for each of these questions, you deem that you have accomplished this step in the process.

4. **Agree to accept a proposal.** Here's a hash mark again. This time, though, we apply a discipline—that they must agree to a specific appointment—at which time you'll present your proposal.

5. **Accept a proposal.** Alas, just because they said they would doesn't mean that they will. You decide to keep track of the dollar volume and number of proposals you make per month.

6. **Sign a contract.** This is a no-brainer. Same as number 5. You decide to keep track of the dollar volume and number of contracts you sign, per month.

Now that you have decided on the key activities for your selling system, and created a way to measure each, you must now create a way to manage the quantity and quality of these activities. So, you create a spreadsheet, or maybe a larger version of it on a whiteboard hanging in your office. On it, you create columns for each week, each month, and then rows for each of the measurements.

Our coffee shop spreadsheet looks like this:

Coffee Shop					
	Week #1	Week #2	Week #3	Week #4	Month
Entered Store					
Approached Drive Up					
Total					
First Cup					
Repeat Visit					
Something Additional					
Email					

Now, you must actually make the measurements. Create some forms, train your staff, and start collecting information. Then, after you have collected sufficient information, at least once a month sit down and analyze what you have. Think in terms of quantity and quality.

Let's fast forward to the end of the first month for the coffee shop selling situation, analyze the numbers, and see what we can learn.

	Coffee Shop				
	Week #1	Week #2	Week #3	Week #4	Month
Entered Store	700	900	650	1100	3350
Approached Drive Up	300	210	160	310	980
Total	1,000	1,100	810	1,410	5,310
First Cup	700	610	426	650	2,346
Repeat Visit	10	30	60	100	200
Something Additional	95	110	86	120	411
Email	30	26	20	20	34

Before we start to think deeply about what it tells us, we need to note one thing. In this example, we are using weekly measurements, and then consolidating them into a monthly number. If it would be useful we could compare the numbers each day, instead of each week. We could also, if we were so inclined, actually compare the numbers for every hour of the day. For now, however, we are just going to use the weekly/monthly numbers.

Let's start our analysis by asking a big question: "Are we achieving our revenue goals?" Our total revenues for the month was $5,500. Because our plan called for a total of $7,000 in revenue, the answer is no.

So, now we have to figure out why. We begin by looking at the quantity. The question we ask now is "Are we doing enough of the right things (key activities)?"

We had 1,500 people come in or stop by the drive in. Let's divide that number into the total revenue and we get a dollar per initial contact of $3.67. So, if we want to have $7,000 in revenue, we either have to get more people to stop in, or get more money from each contact.

We decide to work on both fronts. First, we are going to focus on increasing the quantity of people who come in. So, we are going to look at all the decisions we made about getting people's attention and enticing them to stop in, and see if we can't do them better.

This leads us to revisit the street sign. Maybe if we added color? Let's try that. And that flyer that we distributed to the office buildings—maybe we could print a coupon on it that would entice people to come in. One of the local radio stations has a deal where they will broadcast from your location for a certain fee. We decide to investigate that option.

Notice what is happening here. Because we broke our sales process down into key activities and measured those activities, we are able to focus our time and resources on those specific processes that will yield the greatest response.

> **Using the system concepts enables us to focus our time and resources on those specific processes that will yield the greatest response.**

This provides us a powerful, sustainable way to successfully meet what might be the greatest challenge to sustaining an effective selling effort through time: We must continually change, and change in positive, effective ways, to mesh with the continually changing market.

When we implement this system, and stick to it with discipline, we will have created a continuously evolving solution to the challenge of continuous improvement. Not only that, but by focusing our attention and resources on specific processes, we prevent squandering of time and effort and become much more effective.

In selling, you are never as good as you can be, either individually or systematically. You can always do everything better. By focusing on that one step in the process, you'll come up with some ways to do it better.

> **In selling, you are never as good as you can be, either individually or systematically. You can always do everything better.**

So, in our example, we have taken some steps to increase the quantity of people coming into the system.

Now, let's look more closely at the quality of the system. Your $3.67 per person is a measurement of the effectiveness of your entire system. In other words, it is the quality measurement. If, for example, you generated $5 per person, your sales system would be more effective, or higher quality, than it was before.

Not only can you measure the quality of the total system, but you will find it very helpful to measure the quality of individual steps in the system.

In order to do that, you measure the relationship between two rows on the spreadsheet. For example, when you compare the relationship between the number of people who stopped in, and the number who bought more than one thing, you find that it is 3350:411. In other words, for every one person who bought more than one thing, you had to entice 8.15 in to the store. Your 3350 to 411 ratio converts to a quality measurement of 12 percent (divide one number by the other = a percentage). If you could focus on doing that step better, you could improve that step in the sales process. So, let's say you decide to create a little glass box and sit it on the counter next to the register. You train the wait staff to always put a muffin in it, and then say to every customer: "We have a special today on fresh, homemade muffins." Point to the muffin and say, "Would you like one?"

You do that for a week, and measure the results. Now you see that 18 percent of the people are buying more than one thing. You have improved that step of the process. You are doing it better!

You can duplicate this process with every step of the sale process, and you should. By methodically measuring each key activity, and then reflecting on the quantity and quality of each step in the process, you will regularly identify the weakest spots in your process. By focusing your time and attention on those weak links, you will gradually improve them through time, making your sales system more effective.

This process of measuring the quantity and quality of each step of the sales process needs to be a rigid discipline. Put in place the system of measuring, and then set aside a time each month to reflect on it. Every month, identify some aspect of the system that needs to be improved.

Let's go through the same exercise with the one-on-one selling situation—our freelance grant writer. You have identified some key activities in your selling system. They are:

- Accept a phone call from me and agree to an appointment.
- Articulate the need for additional funds.
- Agree to accept a proposal.
- Accept a proposal.
- Sign a contract.

Because you have a longer selling cycle, you decide to measure the first two months of activities, and your spreadsheet looks like this:

Free Lancer					
	Week #1	Week #2	Week #3	Week #4	Month
Appointments	2	3	0	5	10
Completed Need Form	1	2	0	5	8
Agree to Proposal	1	2	0	4	7
Accept a Proposal	0	0	1	1	2
Number	0	0	1	1	2
$ Volume	0	0	$5,000	$1,000	$6,000
Contract					
Number	0	0	0	1	1
$ Volume	0	0	0	$5,000	$5,000

We'll go through the same disciplines as we did with the mass selling situation at the coffee shop. First, we ask about the end: "Are we achieving our revenue goals?" In this case, you wanted to capture contracts equivalent to $7,000 in billings by the end of the second month. You didn't. Okay. That leads you to the next question: "Are we doing enough of the right things?"

Let's start at the end. You got 10 people to agree to an appointment. That's the first measurable event in your system. Your system generated $5,000 in billable revenue, or $500 per agreement.

So, in order to reach your goals, you must either get more people into your system, or get more money per person.

Your first conclusion is that 10 people for two months of work is not going to be sufficient. Your first priority, then, is to figure out a way to get more people engaged with you.

You make that decision and set it aside for the moment, because you want to see what else you can learn about the strengths and weaknesses of your system.

You noticed that your ratio of closed contracts to proposals is pretty good: 2:1. In other words, you closed 50 percent of the proposals you made. That's a great start. But you only generated two proposals. That's not so good. You noticed, too, that the average dollar volume of your proposals was only $3,000. That means that you would have to close more than two a month if you are going to reach your revenue goals. Working backward, that means that you would have to generate four proposals per month, or generate bigger proposals.

You decide to focus on both. The fact that you closed 50 percent of your proposals indicates that maybe you are a little low on your price. While two proposals isn't enough information to come to a firm conclusion, it is a bit of an indication. So, you decide to increase your billing rate to increase the size of the proposals.

Next, you decide to focus on the front end of the system. If you can get more people to meet with you, you'll generate more proposals, and you'll come closer to reaching your revenue goals.

The actual remedies that you come up with are not that important in this example. If you come up with a fix, and it doesn't work, it will be apparent when you measure it next. So, you go at it again. If your fix does work, great; that too will be apparent when you measure next.

What is important is that you apply the discipline of regularly measuring and fine-tuning your system.

Notice that the discipline of "seeing it as a system" led you to focus on the weakest parts of your system and apply your energies where they will bring the greatest return.

As you implement this discipline of measuring, analyzing, and prioritizing monthly refinements in your system, you will eventually figure it out and be successful. That is, of course, the ultimate goal.

Note: We have assembled a variety of resources to help you accomplish this step of the process. Visit *http://www.sellanythingtoanyone.net/system.php* to review them.

How to Implement the Ideas in This Chapter

1. Create a list of no more than seven key activities.
2. Develop an easy, objective way to measure each.
3. Implement the system and begin to measure each key activity.
4. Create the discipline of reviewing these measurements every month.

- Look at the total output, relative to your goals.
- Look at the quantity of activities.
- Look at the quality of activities.
- Select one or two of the weakest points in the system on which to focus and improve.

15

Seeing Your Sales as a System

Can we take it up a notch? Of course. When it comes to selling, we can always do everything better.

Here's a way to look at your system that will provide you with a tool to use to make every aspect of it better. Those of you who have engineering in your background will find this next idea particularly attractive.

Let's flow-chart the steps in our selling system. This will help us to understand what the customer goes through. Flow charting the process allows us to consider each of the customer's decision points and then to focus precisely on improving the quality of that step in the process. It provides us with an additional layer of insight into the workings of our sales system and helps us to identify the weak spots in the system graphically and with more precision. That, of course, leads us to refinements that will be more highly focused.

First, our legend. A diamond is a point in the process where the prospect/customer has to make a decision. A rectangle is something we do. The hexagon is the customer's actions.

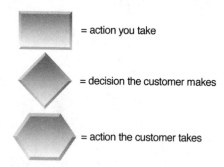

= action you take

= decision the customer makes

= action the customer takes

Let's begin by focusing on our coffee shop, and flow chart the selling process for it. First, we have to get the attention of the right people. We do that by our on-the-street sign, and by distributing flyers in the office park down the street.

Our flow chart begins with our actions:

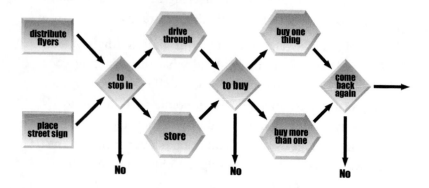

As a result of our initiating the action, the customer decides to stop into the shop. Notice that some do, and some don't. At each decision point along the way, some prospects and customers opt out of the system. Those that remain in our system make a series of positive decisions: to come into the store, to examine the signs, to note the "feel" of the place, and decide to order something. Some do, and some don't.

Before we go on, let's further expand on a point from the last chapter. We emphasized measuring certain key events in the sales process. Now, we want to do it better. The more precisely we can measure the sales system, the more precisely we can refine it, and the more effective it can become.

> **The more precisely we can measure the sales system, the more precisely we can refine it, and the more effective it can become.**

If we chose to we could measure every spot on the process so far. We can measure the number of cars passing our street sign, and compare it to the number of people who stopped in. We could measure the number of people in each office building and the number of flyers we dropped off. And compare that to the number of people who came into the store. Would those measurements be 100-perfect accurate? No, but they would give us good, workable numbers on which to base our decisions and our actions. Now we can precisely target the effectiveness of our first messages. If the ratio is 30:1—that is, for every 30 flyers we handed out, one person came in—can we make some changes in the flyers that will produce a 25:1 ratio? If one person makes that sharp right-hand turn into our location for every 100 cars that pass by, we can ask the question, "What can we do to get one of every 75?"

To continue on with our measuring, we can measure the number of people who buy something, and compare it to the number of people who enter the shop. That would give us an indication of how effective our interior signage was and the "feel" of the shop. We could also measure the number of people who bought more than one thing.

Finally, we could add one more step in the process. How many of them come back? We can measure that, and compare it to the number of people who buy the first time. Let's say our number is 10:1. The question we ask ourselves is, "How can we get more of our customers to come back again?"

Let's apply the same principles and processes to the task of flow-charting the process for our freelance one-on-one selling situation. This is much simpler.

Although the flow chart is simpler, the principles remain the same. You can measure every decision point and make a judgment about how well you are influencing people to make that decision positively. For example, if you call 20 people for an appointment and get one, then your ratio is 20:1. You decide that is not good enough. So, you look at what you are doing in the phone call and see if you can improve it. Once again, flow-charting the process allows you to consider each of the customer's decision points and then to focus precisely on improving the quality of that step in the process.

Let's continue this example. You decide you must improve your phone call, asking for an appointment. You do a little research, find a couple resources on the internet, buy an audio lesson on it, and read a few articles. Then you work on sharpening your script so that it sounds more persuasive.

What you did was use the flow-charting method to identify the weakness in the system, focused your time and energy on improving that one piece of the process, and created a more effective tool (a better script). You will become more effective. You will become successful.

But we have introduced a new term in the last paragraph: *tools*. I'm using the term in a much larger way than the hammer or wrench that the word may first conjure up. A tool is anything you use to help you accomplish a step in the sales process.

> **A tool is anything you use to help you accomplish a step in the sales process.**

The script is a good example, as is the flyer for the coffee shop, the form that you use to hash mark the number of people who come into the shop, and the chalkboard that you write your daily specials on, and so on.

One additional way to add power to your system is to continually review and refine the effectiveness of the tools that you use.

Create tools by asking yourself, "What do I need at this particular point in the process to help me do this?"

Here's a list of the tools that you may create if you are the freelancer:

1. The letterhead on which you create your letter of introduction.
2. The font, size, and color of the type face that you used in the letter.
3. The business card that you print and leave.
4. The script that you created to ask for an appointment.
5. The binder with your credentials that you use in the first appointment.
6. The format that you use, including the language, in your proposal.
7. The contract that is signed when someone hires you.

Looking at the list, you can clearly come to the conclusion that the quality and effectiveness of your tools can dramatically impact the results of your system.

This process of continually and methodically reviewing your results—every step of the process—identifying the weaknesses and focusing on improving the process and the tools, is the key to forever improving your system.

> **This process of continually and methodically reviewing your results—every step of the process—identifying the weaknesses and focusing on improving the process and the tools, is the key to forever improving your system.**

It would be great if you had an unlimited amount of time and money to spend on this process. The reality is, however, that few people or companies do. In fact, if your sales system is going to be effective and *efficient*, it should cost you only a certain amount.

Again, let's establish some terms. Gross profit is the sales price of your product or service, less the cost of producing or acquiring that product or service (cost of goods sold). So, if you charge $2.50 for a latte, and that costs you $.25 for the coffee and water, $.10 for the cup, and $.50 for the server's time, your total direct cost of the product is $.85. Because you sell it for $2.50, your gross profit is $1.65. That's not your bottom-line net profit. Out of that amount you have to pay for the store, the advertising, the lights, and so on. It's the gross profit, not the net profit.

For most products, you should be able to easily calculate a cost of goods sold, and therefore, a gross profit. Services, such as your proposal writing service, are usually somewhat harder to determine. What is your cost, for example, to write that proposal? If you pay yourself an hourly wage, say $30 an hour, and calculate the time you have into the project, multiply it by that number, and you'll have something you can work with that approximates a cost of goods sold. That will allow you to create an estimated gross profit.

Why bother? Because that is the core number to use to assess the efficiency of your sales system. If you spend too much of the gross profit on your sales system, you will probably not be profitable. If you spend too little, you will likely not grow your business. There is a sweet spot when it comes to how much of your gross profit your sales system should cost.

What's the magic number? Calculating the cost of sales systems is a regular exercise at my company, as we work with clients and help them grow their businesses. Through the years, we have computed that number for hundreds of clients—enough that I can be certain as to where the magic spot is. If you have sales of less than $20MM per year, then the magic spot is 30 percent +/- 4 percent. In other words, your sales system should cost you somewhere between 26 percent and 34 percent of your gross profit.

Let's work this out in the coffee shop. For one month, you determine that you had $7,000 in gross profit.

Now, let's figure out the cost of our sales system. The sign, depreciated during three years, costs you $20 a month in depreciation. The electricity for the sign you estimate at $5 per month. The flyers, including design, printing, and the cost of the teenagers to distribute them, were $1,200. Your in-store signage costs you $10 a month. You figure in the time it took to train your servers to do the "sales" stuff that you asked them to do. That was $1,000, amortized over 12 months, or $84 a month. You figure that 10 percent of the server's time is devoted to selling, and 90 percent to fulfilling the orders. So, you add in an allocation of $1,000 for that. Oh, what about your time? Another $1,000.

Let's add it all up. We come to costs of the sales system for that month of $3,319. Now, let's divide that by our $7,000 gross profit. That's 47.4 percent. Yikes! If we keep that up, we'll sell our way out of business.

You can stand that for a month or two, depending on your cash reserves, but you'll need to work that number down to the acceptable range if you are going to be successful in the long run.

The point is this: You can come up with the most creative ways of accomplishing each step in the process, but they must, like every piece of the system, eventually pay for themselves.

The cold reality is every idea, tool, and technique must stand the test of its cost relative to the gross profit it produces. It is one thing to be able to sell something, and it's another to be able to sell it profitably!

We call this formula for creating a financial measurement "Kahle's Kalculation." If you'd like to dig into it deeper, you can get a free download of the concept, specific step-by-step directions, and a spreadsheet by visiting *http://www.davekahle. com/freesalestrainingresources.html.*

In all of this, you may have sensed a foundational principle lurking between the lines of this entire book: Our words and our actions influence the customer's decisions. If we change our words and our actions, we can positively influence the customer's decision.

Our words and our actions influence the customer's decisions. If we change our words and our actions, we can positively influence the customer's decisions.

It may seem late in the game to point out this simple, foundational truth of selling, but it is so often overlooked. The world is full of salespeople, entrepreneurs, freelancers, and sales executives who blame everyone else for their results, and never really "get it"—that their results are *their* results—the direct response of their efforts. If you are not happy with your results, change your actions. These systems disciplines—measuring key activities, flow-charting the processes, regularly reviewing and refining the system—provide you tools to continually improve your actions and, therefore, your results. The steps in the Kahle Way Sales Process are proven observations of how you sell anything to anyone, any-time. If you implement the ideas in this book, you will be successful.

Go forth and sell well!

Note: We have assembled a variety of resources to help you accomplish this step of the process. Visit *http://www. sellanytingtoanyone.net/better.php* to review them.

How to Implement the Ideas in This Chapter

1. Create a flow chart of your sales process, using the tools and symbols described in this chapter.
2. You will find it helpful to have someone else look at it and interpret it, just to make sure you have it right.
3. Identify the decision points along the way, and add measurements for each of the decision points that you can.
4. Add the review of this information to your month-ly reviews.
5. Download the free white paper: How to Kreate Kahle's Kalculation from my Website at *http:// www.davekahle.com/freesalestrainingresources.html*.
6. Create your version of Kahle's Kalculation.
7. Review that number monthly and make refine-ments as necessary.
8. Go forth and sell well!

Glossary

Benefits: The name for the impact features have on the customer.

Capable: The quality of being able to do what you claim you can do.

Collateral: Marketing literature and electronic media that support the sales effort.

Credible: The view, in the mind of the prospect/customer, that your claims are convincing and trustworthy.

Customer: Someone, or some entity, who has given you money for what you offer.

Effectiveness: The measurement of a step in the process, or of the total process, which answers the question: "How well is this effort doing what I want it to do?"

Efficiency: The measurement of a step in the process, or of the total process, which answers the question: "To what degree is it costing us an appropriate amount?"

Entertaining: The practice of creating ways to spend time outside of the business setting with your customers.

Features: The name for the describable characteristics of your offer.

Focus group: A small group of prospects/customers who come together under the sponsorship of a vendor to discuss and provide input on an issue presented by the vendor.

Gross profit: The sales price of your product or service, less the cost of producing or acquiring that product or service.

Kahle's Kalculation: A formula for measuring the productivity of your sales system, as well as parts of the system.

Key activities: Those things that you do—events that you create—that are essential to the successful completion of the sales process.

Leverage: The strategy of using something to create or enlarge something else. In sales, it refers to using a successful transaction to uncover other opportunities.

Macro-environment: The physical elements surrounding the presentation.

Match: The process of precisely aligning the specifics of your offer to the needs and wants of the prospect/customer.

Micro-environment: The place your customer looks at during your presentation.

Partner: A customer who trusts you, believes you consistently bring value to him, sees you and your company as an integral part of his business, and buys almost everything he can from you.

Proof: The specific expressions of the principle that it is always more effective to have someone else say something positive about you than it is for you to do so yourself.

Prospect: Someone, or some entity, who has a legitimate need for your product or service, has the ability to make the decision to buy it, and has the money to pay for it. A prospect, however, has never previously done business with you.

Rapport: The sense on the part of the prospect/customer that you share similar values, feelings, and beliefs with him.

Risk: The idea in the mind of the prospect/customer of what will him happen to him and his company if he makes a mistake in the buying decision.

ROF call: The sales call made after the product has been purchased and implemented by the customer.

Sales call: An interaction between a sales person and a prospect or customer in which the purpose is to come to an agreement for the action that each will take.

Sales system: The sum total of all of your efforts, including the processes, people, principles, and tools, used to bring people from apathy and ignorance to becoming a partner with you.

Survey: A device to collect quantifiable information from a market.

TOMA (Top of Mind Awareness): Practices you employ to keep your name, your company's name, or your products, on the customer's mind so that, when the time comes for him to buy again, he thinks first of you.

Tools: Anything you use to help you accomplish a step in the sales process.

Touches: Light, non-intensive communications from or about you to your company that spotlight your name and keep you at the top of their minds.

Index

About the Author

Dave Kahle is one of America's leading sales educators. He was the number-one sales person in the nation for two different companies in two distinct selling situations. Since 1988, he has served as president of The DaCo Corporation. In that capacity, he has worked one-on-one with more than 251 companies, helping them grow their sales and develop their people.

He's trained tens of thousands of salespeople to be more effective, written nine books, and spoken in 47 states, five Canadian provinces, and seven countries.

He and his wife, Coleen, split their time between Grand Rapids, Michigan, and Sarasota, Florida. They are the parents of five children and eight grandchildren. Dave is a father, foster father, grandfather, and adoptive father.

Visit his Website (*www.davekahle.com*), where you can join one of his groups on LinkedIn, receive his free weekly Ezine, *Thinking about Sales*, become a fan on Facebook, and follow him on Twitter.

Other Works by Dave Kahle

Ten Secrets of Time Management for Sales People (Career Press)

This may be the best-selling time management book for salespeople ever written. This book provides powerful, practical insights and ideas that really work, including hundreds of specific, practical, effective time management tips from dozens of sales people who are on the "front lines" every day.

Question Your Way to Sales Success (Career Press)

A good question is the sales person's single most powerful tool, one that can be powerfully used in every stage of the sales process, from making appointments to closing the sale to following up afterward; yet, most salespeople are ill-equipped to use this powerful tool effectively. As a result, they find themselves dealing with "price" issues, and wondering why the customer purchased from someone else.

Question Your Way to Sales Success transforms the way you think and operate by offering specific, practical advice on how to ask "better sales questions."

Visit *www.davekahle.com* to review a selection of books, podcasts, Webinars, online courses, and other resources by the author.

Visit *www.howtosellanythingtoanyone.net* to review resources specific to the content of this book.